BFI TV Classics

BFI TV Classics is a series of books celebrating key individual television programmes and series. Television scholars, critics and novelists provide critical readings underpinned with careful research, alongside a personal response to the programme and a case for its 'classic' status.

Cathy Come Home

Stephen Lacey

A BFI book published by Palgrave Macmillan

First published in 2011 by
PALGRAVE MACMILLAN

on behalf of the

BRITISH FILM INSTITUTE
21 Stephen Street, London W1T 1LN
www.bfi.org.uk

There's more to discover about film and television through the BFI. Our world-renowned archive, cinemas, festivals, films, publications and learning resources are here to inspire you.

PALGRAVE MACMILLAN in the UK is an imprint of Macmillan Publishers Limited, registered in England, company number 785998, of Houndmills, Basingstoke, Hampshire RG21 6XS. Palgrave Macmillan in the US is a division of St Martin's Press LLC, 175 Fifth Avenue, New York, NY 10010. Palgrave Macmillan is the global academic imprint of the above companies and has companies and representatives throughout the world. Palgrave® and Macmillan® are registered trademarks in the United States, the United Kingdom, Europe and other countries.

Set by Cambrian Typesetters, Camberley, Surrey
Printed in China

This book is printed on paper suitable for recycling and made from fully managed and sustained forest sources. Logging, pulping and manufacturing processes are expected to conform to the environmental regulations of the country of origin.

British Library Cataloguing-in-Publication Data

A catalogue record for this book is available from the British Library

ISBN 978-1-84457-316-5

Contents

Introduction

In what sense is *Cathy Come Home* a TV classic? The question seems somehow impertinent. *Cathy* has been central to television history for so long that its canonical status is beyond question and appears to be hardly worth revisiting, even if the film itself is still worth our attention. There are many different ways of thinking about the term 'classic', of course. It is notoriously slippery and controversial, equally at home in the critical discourses of the high and popular arts and in the currency of everyday conversation, ubiquitous, but, in an age of cultural relativism, not always respectable. Certainly, the accretions of value and judgment that the term has acquired can sometimes short circuit discussion rather than focus it. Like other terms with which it is sometimes associated, such as 'canon' or 'landmark', it shelters complex histories and ideologies from view. Yet, these caveats notwithstanding, the questions that 'classic' poses for us do not disappear if we stop using it; questions of history, aesthetic value, political intent and effect/affect, influence – these remain important, and 'the classic' is one way of prising them open.

I am fortunate to be able to write this Introduction in the wake of a one-day symposium at the University of Warwick entitled 'Making and Remaking Television Classics',[1] in which this current series was, a little hazily, in the spotlight. The definition of 'classic' used in the commissioning of the series was succinctly stated by the commissioning editor, Rebecca Barden. I am giving my take on her criteria here, for which I hope she will forgive me. A 'Classic TV' programme should be all or some of the following: important to the history of the form; critically acclaimed and have had an impact (on what is open to interpretation, but on television as a minimum); significant in the development of the genre in which it sits; be innovative within and perhaps against that genre; popular (by which I take to mean have had some demonstrable presence in television history and to have been seen by large numbers of people); likely to be on television studies syllabi (an important part of the readership); available on DVD. To this should be added typicality, the classic as the best example of a general phenomenon. By all but one of these criteria, *Cathy Come Home* would seem to qualify. (It is, alas, no longer available on DVD, although the 2003 BBC Worldwide release can still be found, and there are so many copies of the drama in circulation, mostly on VHS, that finding a copy to view is not normally a problem.)

There are few television dramas that have quite the same presence in British culture. *Cathy*'s exposure of the realities of the post-war housing crisis led directly to changes in government policy (the ending of the separation of men from their families in hostels for the homeless) and is credited with being partly responsible for the success of the housing charity Shelter (see Chapter 4). It is also one of the most repeated of programmes, having been broadcast on six separate occasions to date (1966, 1967, 1968, 1976, 1993 and 2006). From the moment of its first transmission on 16 November 1966, it was clear that *Cathy Come Home* was different, and this was reflected in the press coverage (see Chapter 4). Indeed, for a time, the reputation of television itself was dependent on its success. As Edward Lucie-Smith commented in 1971, five years after its first appearance, 'If you want to defend the medium to its detractors, mention *Cathy Come Home*.'[2] *Cathy* has been almost universally applauded, at the time and since, its importance recognised even by critics who are a little suspicious of its methods. In 2000, the BFI commissioned a survey of 1,600 members of the television industry, inviting them to nominate the most 'important, influential and innovative' television programmes of all time (not only drama). The result, *The BFI TV 100*, placed *Cathy Come Home* at number two,

tucked in just behind *Fawlty Towers* (BBC 1975–9). In 2007, Channel 4
transmitted *50 Greatest TV Dramas* based on a list of US and UK
dramas compiled by television professionals and (some) academics (the
'list programme' is now a staple of the schedules and is one of the ways
that television's history is recovered and circulated). *Cathy* came in at
number five (*The Sopranos* (HBO 1999–2007) won outright, with *Boys
from the Blackstuff* (BBC 1980–2), *Edge of Darkness* (BBC 1985) and
The Singing Detective (BBC 1986) – the latter two the subject of other
volumes in this series – in rank order above it[3]). Given the shortness of
memory of even television professionals, this is still not bad for a black-
and-white drama from the 1960s, shot on a small budget in three weeks.

Indeed, our cultural memory of television is, as Caughie
observes, much more limited and generational than of cinema.[4] It is,
simply, difficult to rely on audiences – even students, who might be
expected to be interested in such things – being aware of dramas of even
ten years ago, although the profusion of digital channels broadcasting
programmes from other eras is changing this in certain ways. This
relative lack of a known and easily recalled history works against that
sense of a classic that relies on an awareness of the importance of a
programme in a synchronic history of television drama. As Christine
Geraghty has recently observed, 'the categorisation of "the classic" in
which quality is proved by longevity works against the emphasis of
television (and television studies) on the contemporary'.[5] Longevity is
certainly important to a programme's classic status, since durability,
however achieved, is a marker of quality. It is also important to the way
that a drama relates to its genre(s). While that relationship may be
obvious at the moment of transmission, it may also require time before a
settled view appears. Time may serve to remove a programme from its
association with a specific genre, and there is a tension between that
sense of a classic that connotes typicality and that which connotes
distinctiveness, which is never finally resolvable. More often, however,
the relationship between a classic and its genre is redefined, as genres
change, adapt and hybridise, leaving a drama that once seemed a
harbinger of a new form seeming an experimental oddity (I will argue

3

below that this is what has happened to *Cathy Come Home* in relation to documentary-drama).

What genre does *Cathy Come Home* belong to? It is certainly thought to exemplify the single play at its best, although this is not a genre as such, but rather a programme format. The single play is itself historical, in that it is now very rare to have a television drama defined as a 'play', television's associations with theatre having long since been shaken off, an uneven and incomplete process to which *Cathy* contributed. In the mid-1960s, *Cathy Come Home* was described as a play, but this was already looking problematic, as contemporary reviewers suggested (see Chapter 4). In recognition of the difficulty of classifying it, I have referred to *Cathy* throughout this book as a play, film and drama, in what I confess is a deliberately unsystematic way: it can be thought of as all three, and the implications of each way of seeing it are confronted in the analysis rather than in the use of the terms themselves. Similarly, single dramas/films of any kind are no longer the staple of the schedules that they were. Once the backbone of the drama output of the BBC in particular, the single play – that is, a one-off drama branded as a 'play' rather than a drama/film – disappeared with the demise of Play for Today in 1984, and even the single film is an infrequent presence. As David Hare, a notable contributor to Play for Today (BBC 1970–84), recently observed, 'mention of the single play, in which one writer is given the opportunity to make his or her own fiction at will, seems to evoke the past more powerfully than Green Shield Stamps or Craven A'.[6] (If the references are not understood, then the point is made even more powerfully.)

The single play still occupies a distinct place in the history of television drama in the UK. Writing of The Wednesday Play (BBC 1964–70), the anthology series most identified with the single play in its heyday and in which *Cathy Come Home* was transmitted, Lez Cooke summarised the position thus:

> It is often seen as synonymous with a 'golden age' in British television
> drama, an age when playwrights had the freedom to experiment and

regularly produced innovative drama, when there were not the commercial
pressures to capture and retain audiences that were later to become such
important factors in television, and when it was possible to engage with the
pressing social issues of the day and provide argument and discussion,
even social change, through the medium of the single play.[7]

Talk of a 'golden age', as Cooke later notes, is always to be treated with
circumspection, even though there is clearly some truth in the
mythology (which is what makes it so persistent). Cooke captures this
effectively: the single play as the site of author-led, socially aware and
contemporary drama that was also frequently experimental in form. It
represented, in David Hare's view, 'the most important new indigenous
art form of the 20th century'.[8]

    Cathy Come Home's classic status rests on it not only
representing the single play in its full glory, but also creating it in a
specific sense. *Cathy* demonstrated what the single play could be and
could do, its singular achievements seeming to encompass the
possibilities of the form. It is, perhaps, for this reason that the drama
continues to have such a presence on the syllabi of television drama
courses and why it has such a commanding presence in the narrative
history of television studies. Of course, caveats need to be entered at
once: *Cathy* did not do this single-handedly, and the single play at this
time would have been important and worth our attention even without
it. The list of people associated with the two main single play strands at
the BBC, The Wednesday Play and its successor Play for Today, includes
many of the most important writers, directors and producers working in
television then and since: writers such as Dennis Potter, David Mercer,
Alan Bleasdale, David Rudkin, David Hare and Alan Plater; directors
such as Alan Clarke, Stephen Frears, Michael Apted, Ken Loach and
Mike Leigh; producers such as Tony Garnett, Irene Shubik and Ken
Trodd. Also, the success of the single play was the result of considerable
struggle, both within the BBC and outside it.[9]

    The development of the single play will form a sub-theme in
this book, but there are two further points to make by way of

5

introduction. First, the term 'single play' was always a misnomer, strictly speaking, since each individual play relied for its influence in part on its place in the anthology series of which it was located. Both The Wednesday Play and Play for Today had a distinct identity – again, partly created by *Cathy* – which shaped the commissioning process, the production values and critical and viewer expectations. The anthology series, therefore, attempted to combine the variety and experimentation of the one-off drama with the brand identity of the series. Second, *Cathy Come Home* is not evidence of the model of single play production that Hare and others implicitly promote, where each drama was the direct product of a single, authorial viewpoint (the writer's). It was not an auteurist project. Instead, it is a moment where the collaborative potential of television drama production was in evidence (see Chapter 2), with director, producer and writer working in ways that are impossible to disentangle.

 I do not remember seeing *Cathy Come Home* when it was first screened, although I would have been a teenager (just). I am told that I probably did see it, since we used, as a family, to watch Wednesday Plays as a matter of course (my mum can still, in her eighties, recall the effect of the film's ending on her). We were responding, like many other families, to the ways in which The Wednesday Play, and television generally, brought the wider world into our living room. A respondent to an online forum catches the excitement of the educative potential of television as it emerged as the dominant mass medium:

> As an adolescent, television plays had a stimulating effect on my imagination and my view of the world. Those plays introduced me to ideas and people I would never have been exposed to in my small working class village of 50 years ago.[10]

 This is one reason why a consideration of *Cathy Come Home*'s production and reception contexts will be important to this book. One side effect of the discourses around the 'classic' is the tendency to remove a text from the historical moment in which it appeared, but this would skew our sense of why *Cathy* was significant. It was, for example, immediately popular with its audience, with 12 million people viewing it in November 1966 and the same number two months later in January 1967. The BBC's audience research indicated unprecedented levels of appreciation (see Chapter 4). It was also produced at a time when the rules of engagement, as it were, were being written between programme-makers and their audiences, and when the dominant conventions of television drama were being formed (see Chapter 1). Part of the response to *Cathy* was because it was the first time that the workings of the welfare state had been so devastatingly exposed in dramatic form, and some of the fiercest critics of the film were officials charged with making the system work. There were also only three television channels, and the brutal realities of multi-channel audience fragmentation had yet to emerge. As Ken Loach gently reminds us in the commentary to the DVD, these were more innocent times.

Cathy Come Home has also been important to the development of one of the most controversial forms of television, although it is best thought of as a field of enquiry rather than a single form: the documentary-drama, or drama-documentary. Clearly, *Cathy* uses documentary techniques to tell its dramatic story, and this was one of the reasons why it was both controversial and effective. However, it has not been widely imitated, and most docudrama or dramadoc has gone in different directions, leaving *Cathy* as untypical in the ways in which it inserts documentary directly into the dramatic frame. The film's makers did not repeat the experiment. Director Ken Loach and producer Tony Garnett formed a long and close relationship, working together successfully in both television and cinema between the mid-1960s and the late 1970s. They moved, however, away from docudrama hybrids towards more standard social-realist dramas shot with the kind of observational camerawork that is familiar to audiences of Loach's later cinema films. The four-part *Days of Hope* (BBC 1975) and the cinema film *Kes* (1969) are the best examples of their work in this period. Similarly, *Cathy Come Home*'s writer, Jeremy Sandford, who never worked with Loach and Garnett again, had one more success with

Edna, the Inebriate Woman (BBC 1971). Based on his research into homelessness and ageing, *Edna* won prizes and plaudits, but did not rely on the kind of contextualisation that the documentary techniques used in *Cathy* permitted. In some ways, therefore, the lessons and provocations that *Cathy Come Home* offers have not yet been absorbed, and it remains elusive and hard to place. Though clearly a precursor of sorts to docudrama, it is rooted in a social-realist politics that also draws on *nouvelle vague* cinema, Brecht and British modernist documentary. It points a way forward that is unlikely to receive much of a hearing in the contemporary production climate, in which experiment is constrained within the embrace of familiar genres. It is for this reason, as much as the fact that it is a classic, that it is worth paying attention to.

1 *Cathy Come Home* in Context

Cathy Come Home was broadcast in 1966, an auspicious year in post-war British history, and one of relatively few historical conjunctures where there was a general optimism about the possibilities for change: that this was to be short-lived and based on largely illusory assumptions about progress and prosperity is a sub-theme in the story of *Cathy*'s relationship to its historical context. However, the optimism was genuine enough, and was symbolised by the General Election of that year, which gave Harold Wilson's Labour Government an overall majority of ninety-seven seats (it had come to power two years previously with a majority of only four). Expectations were high, not least because Wilson, a pipe-smoking northerner, identified himself with the age itself, and against the Conservative-dominated years of 1951–64 that preceded it, symbolised by the Edwardian hauteur of Harold McMillan, who had led the Tories from 1956–63, and the aristocratic blandness of Sir Alec Douglas-Home who replaced him. Wilson spoke the language of progress and change, of science and technology (he was the son of an industrial chemist). As John Seed has argued, 'Wilson not only formulated a highly-effective rhetoric of modernisation ... but in his very person seemed to embody it.'[11] This was not the first time that change had figured in the discourses of post-war debate.

British society underwent profound change after the end of World War II and, in the 1950s, this main narrative was of economic growth, social stability and full employment (although it has also been viewed as a period of relative economic decline, as the UK sought to adjust to new post-Imperial realities). The statistics of prosperity – or 'affluence', which became the key term to describe the new situation – are impressive:[12] unemployment hovered around a mere 1–2 per cent throughout the 1950s, while earnings increased by 110 per cent and the standard of living rose by 30 per cent in real terms. Increased wealth was being spent on a range of newly available consumer goods. Car ownership leaped from 2.25–8 million between 1951 and 1964, while sales of fridges, telephones, washing machines more than doubled. Not for the last time, television was central to debates about the nature and meaning of social change. The phenomenal growth in the ownership of television sets through the 1950s and 60s was both a symbol of affluence – and celebrated as such by the popular press and television itself – and a carrier of messages about that affluence. In 1951 there were just 760,000 licensed television sets in the UK, but by 1955 this had risen to 4.5 million and by 1964 to 13 million, which represented 82 per cent of the UK population.[13]

The UK's economic performance looks less impressive when measured against that of our chief competitors (all our major European trading partners saw increases in productivity, exports and wages that were greater than Britain's[14]). In any case, affluence was undoubtedly more selective than the rhetoric suggested, and the statistics conceal regional and social variations: it was also much more easily registered in the ownership of consumer durables, such as TV sets and fridges, than it was in, say, housing – a point *Cathy Come Home* made forcefully. In fact, the contradictions of affluence were felt particularly keenly in the domain of housing. There was significant investment in house-building in the 1950s, with the new Conservative Government making it a priority. By 1954, a target of 300,000 new houses had been passed, and between 1948 and 1958 one in six families had moved into a new house or flat.[15] However, the priority was to support private house building, beginning a process that still continues of creating a 'property-owning democracy'. The proportion of housing being built privately in 1951 was

12 per cent; by 1959, 56 per cent of all house completions were private, mostly in new estates, while the number of new local authority houses had halved since a peak in 1953. One result of this policy, which was motivated by ideology rather than economics, was that slum clearance was a low priority. As Pinto-Duschinsky has pithily expressed it:

> Few of the houses that appeared in their neat rows during the 1950s were earmarked for the inhabitants of Stepney or the Gorbals. The housing programme benefitted the upper echelons of the working class and the middle classes – Conservative voters or potential supporters.[16]

The situation was particularly difficult for people like Cathy and her family who were reliant on the private housing sector. In 1945, with 20 per cent of the housing stock destroyed or badly damaged, some 57 per cent of the population lived in the private rented sector, while only 10 per cent lived in council housing. While the balance had shifted by the early 1960s, controls on private rents were loosened significantly from 1957 onwards, with landlords able to increase rents once the existing tenants had moved out. Some of the worst abuses of the post-war housing system were committed at this time, with some slum landlords creating empires of high-cost, multiple-occupancy housing in the inner cities by forcibly evicting tenants and cramming the vacated houses with many more people, often immigrants, on higher rents. The most notorious of these, Peter Rachman, gave his name to this kind of activity – 'Rachmanism' – and made a fortune before being exposed on his death in 1962. Rachman and his descendents are evoked when Cathy and Reg are evicted from a house, which has fallen into neglect, because the landlord, a shadowy presence represented by an 'agent', is able to argue that he wants the property for his own use.

Amid the optimism of 1966, however, little of this would surface. The main narratives were about national success, in which it seemed that Britain might take its place once more at the head of the international table. As is often the case in significant and over-determined conjunctures such as this, the rhetoric of politics resonates

11

elsewhere in the culture. In addition to Wilson's election success, Britain – or, more precisely, London – was attracting attention as the centre of an international youth culture, one consequence of the rise of affluence across the West. Focused on music (the astonishing success of The Beatles and the Rolling Stones) and clothes (Mary Quant and Carnaby Street), the UK was the hip place to be. This was something Wilson, who arranged to be photographed with The Beatles, understood well. In April that year, *Time* magazine, its antennae acutely attuned to popular culture, placed a cartoon montage on its front cover under the headline 'London: The City that Swings', and led with an editorial that announced that London had replaced New York as the centre of the new youth culture.[17] The phrase 'Swinging London' and its many variants had now been sanctioned. 1966 was also the year that Britain hosted the football World Cup: the national team won the trophy for the first and (to date) only time. The final against Germany, which went to extra time and was won 4–2, was watched by an estimated 400 million people around the world. Its impact in the UK was difficult to overestimate.

12   Taken together, these events offer an imagery of success, defined not in relation to the dour culture of the immediate post-war world, but in relation to 'the new', which was increasingly in the domain of the personal and cultural rather than the economic: abortion under certain conditions was legalised (1967), pre-production theatre censorship was abandoned (1968), racism criminalised (1968), homosexuality (partially) de-criminalised (1967) and capital punishment suspended, prior to abolition (1965). However, this energy was not evenly distributed and, by the end of the decade, the Labour Government appeared exhausted and failing, largely for economic reasons. Success on the football field was equally difficult to sustain. The underlying problems that the imagery of 1966 had no room for had re-emerged, and one of these was the housing crisis. While Sandford was researching *Cathy Come Home*, a Government White Paper of 1965 argued that the housing situation was so bad that 'three million families still live in slums, near slums, or in grossly overcrowded conditions'.[18] The White Paper proposed that 3.7 million dwellings be built

immediately to solve the crisis, and noted that 180,000 would be needed in each year thereafter. This was far in excess of anything that had been attempted at that point, and was quietly ignored. It is at both the problem and official denial of its magnitude that *Cathy Come Home* is addressed.

Television Drama at the BBC: Practices, People and Programmes

In the mid-1960s, the BBC seemed quietly confident, if not smug, about its achievements and pre-eminent position. In Hugh Carlton-Greene, its new director-general, the BBC had someone who seemed well placed to meet the twin challenges of seeing off commercial television and steering the Corporation into the next phase of its development. By the mid-1960s, it had recovered much of the ground it had lost in the late 1950s to its flashier and noisier commercial rival, ITV, especially in the crucial area of drama.[19] It had also been vindicated by the 1962 report of the influential, Government-appointed Pilkington Committee into the future of broadcasting. The BBC's reward was the third channel, BBC2, in 1964, from which arose a new challenge: taken with an expansion of the number of broadcast hours, there was a hugely increased demand for television drama in all its forms.[20] In a very short space of time, the BBC's drama budget increased by 40 per cent.[21]

13

A second challenge to the Corporation was that of defining its role in a society that was changing in significant ways. Under the stern gaze of its founding director-general (1927–38), Sir John Reith, the BBC had interpreted its role as guardian of public service values in traditional ways, and although Reith had claimed an independence from government for the Corporation, it had become identified with the establishment, culturally if not politically. However, it is more accurate to see the BBC not so much as an instrument of traditional values as one of the public arenas in which the struggle between competing ideologies and value-systems was being played out. The requirement of its Charter to educate, entertain and inform would not allow any easy resolution of the resulting tensions.

The expansion of the BBC in the early 1960s brought a new generation of practitioners into British television. Some, like Sydney Newman, who became Head of Drama in 1963, were already experienced television professionals (that Newman was a Canadian with a background in film production for television who was poached from a commercial rival, ABC, was itself an indication of a shift in institutional thinking). Others, like Garnett, Loach and writers John McGrath and Troy Kennedy Martin, brought new expectations of the medium and a left-wing sensibility that was both cultural and political.

Newman's arrival in British television in 1958 as a producer and then supervisor of ABC's prestigious Sunday-night single-drama anthology series Armchair Theatre (1956–68) was an early indication that broadcasters were beginning to look beyond the UK for new ways of making television drama. Armchair Theatre was one of the most innovative series on UK television at the time, bringing new writers to television, such as Alun Owen and Harold Pinter, and giving a platform among its heterogeneous output to contemporary and social-realist drama. It proved popular with audiences, too. Scheduled on a Sunday night after the hugely successful *Sunday Night at the London Palladium* (ATV 1955–67, 1973–4), it inherited some of its audience – a lesson in the importance of scheduling Newman was to remember. The task, as Newman quickly realised, was not just to find new drama to fill the schedules, but, in fact, to overhaul the system. This he did by separating the roles of producer and director and introducing the job of script, or story, editor. The result was a production model that resembled the Hollywood studio system, with creative teams led by a producer.[22]

Newman introduced the same system when he was poached by the BBC, charged by Hugh Carlton-Greene with bringing new writers to television.[23] However, to do this would, he argued, require profound structural change. Newman's first action was to divide BBC Drama into three sections (series, serials and the single play) each with its own head. As at ABC, Newman also separated the roles of director and producer, placing the latter in a pivotal role, and charging script/story editors with the task of developing new drama under the eye of the producer. *Cathy Come Home*'s producer, Tony Garnett, combined both roles, giving him considerable autonomy in discovering, developing and making the kind of drama he wanted. 'The producer was in the driving seat,' he later commented; 'Any higher in the formal hierarchy and you would find yourself in management, removed from the creative work … any lower in the hierarchy and you would find yourself waiting on the end of a telephone, unable to initiate anything.'[24] *Cathy Come Home* was a beneficiary of this relative creative and institutional freedom.

Structural change occurred in the context of considerable debate, much of it partisan and theoretical, about the aesthetics and politics of television drama. This was conducted in boardrooms, pubs and canteens, as well as in the pages of *Contrast* (1961–5), a journal devoted entirely to television, and *Encore* (1957–65), which was closely aligned with New Wave theatre, but which also published material on television. *Contrast*, in particular, was very aware that the recent expansion of the network had created new possibilities that had still to be exploited. The debate about whether television drama was essentially a live medium, most fully itself in the studio, or whether it was film by another name, was particularly ferocious. The commitment to 'liveness' arose out of both technological determinations and the inherited weight of practices that borrowed from the theatre (for example, television writers at the time wrote 'plays', not scripts – and certainly not films).

However, the aesthetics of stage-oriented liveness were under pressure. In 1963, John Maddison asked the question 'What is a Television Film?' and answered it by noting that even in live drama the technical demands were more akin to those of film than theatre, and that any recording technology would accentuate this, since editing would become a factor. In a prescient aside that pointed towards *Cathy Come Home*, Maddison lamented that 'we are still waiting for the fictional film-maker, who will take his cameras into the streets with the same mastery, and an even greater suppleness, than Rossellini did in *Open City*'.[25]

Perhaps the most significant intervention into debates about television drama aesthetics came from the writer Troy Kennedy Martin, whose bracing and articulate polemic against the dominant aesthetic, 'Nats Go Home', was published in *Encore*,[26] a magazine devoted to the new theatre, in Spring 1964. The article, which has been much debated since, proceeded from a diagnosis of the (perilous) state of television drama in the mid-1960s and argued that the principle culprit was 'naturalism', shorthand for studio-bound, dialogue-driven and socially outmoded drama. Constrained by chronological and spatial literalness, naturalist television drama was a 'makeshift bastard born of the theatre and photographed with film techniques ... which can now be seen to be destructive of television'.[27] Even Armchair Theatre-style social realism, he argued, did not challenge the fundamental limitations of the form. The solution was a drama based on narrative and action. At this point, the examples to hand were of studio-based and live drama (Kennedy Martin quotes at length from *The Night of the Long Knives*, a play he had written with John McGrath, but he could easily have included the multi-story, ensemble police series *Z Cars* (BBC 1962–78)).

'Nats Go Home' marked a significant shift in thinking, not least because it stated, implicitly, that the future of television drama lay with film. Tony Garnett, who was among those whose responses to 'Nats Go Home' were published in the following issue of *Encore*, made the case explicitly.

> Once you deny the usefulness of the concept of absolute continuity (the 'live' fiction is taking a long time to die), and admit editing after the event rather than the selection of available shots concurrent with the event, then most people would contend that you were making films. I further suggest that the only useful distinctions between films and television drama arise from the way they are presented and the conditions under which they are experienced; these are the important fields to work in.[28]

In a comment that was to prefigure *Cathy Come Home*'s engagement with television documentary and current affairs, he noted:

> Nearly all the memorable television I have ever seen has been in the fields of documentary, news or plain talk – the Cup Final, Whicker in Mexico, the Nixon–Kennedy confrontation. The shooting of Lee Oswald on television would have satisfied even Zola.

Kennedy Martin and Garnett represented an important, though by no means universally accepted, axis in debates about drama aesthetics. Initially, the aesthetic argument was dominated by the technological one, since electronic transmission did not permit the recording or storing of programmes (at least, not until the mid–late 1950s). Film, in its 35mm format, was used to provide inserts in television plays, but did not replace live transmission (with the exception of popular entertainment series produced by the commercial television companies, such as *The Adventures of Robin Hood* (ABC 1955–9)). 16mm film, the technology of most documentary and current affairs, was unheard of in drama production (see Chapter 2). A process of recording the television image onto screen known as telerecording was available as early as 1947[29] and this was later superseded by videotape, which, despite its initial intractability, eventually dispelled the lingering attractions of live transmission. This was largely because of what it shared with film: it could be more easily controlled in post-production and allowed programmes to become commodities in an increasingly competitive home and international market. It also became cheaper and, as a result, the dominant technology of television drama production during the 1960s. Significantly, videotape was a studio-based technology.

17

Television Realism and The Wednesday Play

The arguments about the relationship of television drama to film were, in a process to which *Cathy Come Home* contributed, largely about location shooting rather than filmed drama in the studio. As Garnett's comments quoted above imply, the film that was worth watching on television, in whatever format, was shot 'out there' beyond the studio. The camera could, as Raymond Williams reminds us, 'move out of the doors into the street, into the public places which on the whole the theatrical drama had left behind'.[30] This was one reason why realism rapidly became important to the discussion.

Realism has been central to post-war culture, the dominant mode of the New Waves in both theatre and cinema in the 1950s and 60s. It is a rich, complex and varied term, capacious in its ability to absorb a variety of forms and intentions; twentieth-century culture has given us social realism, socialist realism, neo-realism (in the cinema), the 'classic realist text' (in film theory), surrealism and magical realism. Realism's transparency, its common-sense familiarity and its ready linkage to the 'immediacy' of television have made it the 'natural' mode of much television drama. On the one hand, realism often connotes mimetic and illusionistic formal methods, with 'truth' of representation equated with the aesthetics of transparency. On the other, it is associated with intention rather than method, with the debate dominated by a position which argues that realism is 'the injection of new content into an orthodox dramatic form'.[31] Yet this has always seemed too simple: new 'content', new dramatic intentions, also reshape inherited dramatic forms, even when that is not the main purpose.

Raymond Williams, whose sustained engagement with realism in its many manifestations has influenced this discussion, has argued that realism is both method and intention, and is best thought of as a tradition of representation that embraces both. In 'A Defence of Realism',[32] Williams offers four criteria by which realism might judged, of which two are of particular importance here. Realism refers, he argues, to drama that engages with the contemporary world, as both setting and subject matter. 'The contemporary' is more than a backdrop but the focus of active investigation; a realist text engages with what it means to be a certain kind of person in a particular time and place, which is, generally speaking, that of its first audience. Realism is also linked to the representation of the social experience of marginalised social groups, especially in class terms (what Williams calls social extension). Indeed, in the post-war cultural context realism has become synonymous with representations of the 'working class', mostly in its contemporary forms, often preceded by 'northern', 'gritty' and 'kitchen sink'. Realism of this kind was not confined to any one dramatic form, and the realist momentum accelerated across novels (*Saturday Night and Sunday Morning, Room at the Top*), plays (*Look Back in Anger, A Taste of Honey*), films (based on these and other realist novels and plays) and eventually television (via ABC's Armchair Theatre and the BBC's The Wednesday Play anthology series).

Realism implies a direct engagement, often in highly mimetic forms, with that which is suppressed, and is associated with the loosening of the ties that bind representation to the norms of a dominant culture, which is one reason why it became important in the 1960s. Social extension, in this way, connotes the breaking of taboos other than those around class – around the representation of sexuality, for example – with considerable effect on post-war culture generally. It is also, by implication, political, in both broad and narrow senses, foregrounding the relationship between individuals and groups and their social environment (see Chapter 2). As Williams notes elsewhere, realist drama reveals the ways in which human beings are 'trapped' by the circumstances in which they find themselves, 'showing a man or woman making an effort to live a much fuller life and encountering the objective limits of a particular social order'.[33] Additionally, television is a significant 'test case' for realist drama, an endpoint of the realist trajectory, with an audience as well as a dramatic action that was now fully socially extended.

Among the new generation of radicals who came to the BBC in the early 1960s, to be a realist carried a moral imperative. Writing of British culture of the time, John Caughie argued this was a combination of political engagement and provincial non-conformism:

> It is a kind of ethical seriousness, rather than simply formal realism, which seems to underpin the cultural movements associated with the 1950s and

19

1960s. This is what gives them much of their power and their value: the sense that these things mattered and that theatre or literature or television drama could do something about them.[34]

Later, Loach and Garnett were to describe this as a 'fidelity to the everyday', a bearing witness to the daily struggles of ordinary people that was inevitably political in its implications. 'The left often forgets to attend to the living details of working class life,' Garnett later argued. 'In our films, however, we see a fidelity to the texture of the everyday as an act of political respect and solidarity.'[35] Such an attitude animates both the methods and intentions of the kind of realism that *Cathy Come Home* embodies, and describes one of the main ambitions of The Wednesday Play.

The Wednesday Play anthology series has acquired a pivotal role in the history of television drama, regarded perhaps nostalgically as a symbol of the kind of author-led, issue-based drama that is no longer on our screens (see Introduction). As MacMurraugh-Kavanagh has observed, from the viewpoint of a de-regulated, multi-channel age, 'it is taken to connote both the Golden Age of British television drama and a lost era of public service vision and integrity'.[36] Many of the most widely discussed and controversial plays of the decade were produced for it (although it sheltered a wide variety of dramas under its wing, with more conventional fare sitting alongside the experimental and provocative).[37]

Commencing in October 1964, The Wednesday Play ran in seasons in a regular Wednesday evening slot on BBC1 until October 1970, when it switched to Thursday and was retitled Play for Today. It was formed out of two existing play strands, Festival and First Night, and was designed to relaunch the single play. Its main producer was James MacTaggart, who produced a number of play anthologies for the BBC in the early 1960s and was an ally of Sydney Newman's and protector of the new radicals. Its character owed much to Newman's desire to create a drama series that would represent contemporary Britain. In a memo to Kenneth Adam, BBC Commissioner of Programmes, in June 1966, eighteen months into its run, Newman argued that The Wednesday Play represented 'the turning points in contemporary Britain' and that audiences 'want to know about the experiences of people in other occupations and classes, and how they face *their* problems which may be similar to their own'.[38] This positioned television drama in terms of its relationship to the concerns of a popular audience and, emphatically, a powerful rhetoric of immediacy, relevance and realism. Elsewhere he accorded the series a more combative role, arguing that its defining characteristic was 'agitational contemporaneity'. The BBC hierarchy were less sure of this purpose, and even when they defended it publicly were often much more circumspect in private.[39]

The first full season of The Wednesday Play ran from January to December 1965, and contained Loach and Garnett's first experiment with 16mm realist dramatic form, *Up the Junction*. Transmitted on 3 November, *Up the Junction* was shot mostly on location and prefigured many of the innovations that are associated with *Cathy Come Home*, including a shooting style informed by documentary (Tony Imi, a documentary cameraman, shot both films) and wild-track sound. (*Up the Junction* was important to the way that *Cathy Come Home* was interpreted, and will be discussed further in Chapter 4.) This season was also the first to show the influence of the new generation of script editors – notably Garnett, along with Ken Trodd (later to become a drama producer) and Roger Smith – committed to seeking out new writers new to television and interested in contemporary themes.[40] Twenty-seven writers contributed thirty-three new plays to this season, thirty-two of which were written specifically for television (Dennis Potter alone contributed four of these).[41]

The 1965 season gave The Wednesday Play its identity as a space for contemporary, realist drama, and this was not due solely to *Up the Junction*. For example, three of the most high-profile plays were on identifiable social issues that resonated more widely. *Fable* (written by John Hopkins) was set in a future in which a black majority exercised power over a white minority and was conceived as a parable about apartheid, while the same author's *Horror of Darkness* dealt with the repression faced by gay men in a society where homosexuality was still

21

criminalised. And James (Jimmy) O'Connor's *Three Clear Sundays* was a well-received indictment of capital punishment (O'Connor had himself once been convicted of murder). Like *Up the Junction* in relation to the issue of abortion, both *Horror of Darkness* and *Three Clear Sundays* were conceived as contributions to debates that were to lead to legislation (homosexuality between consenting adults in private was legalised in 1967 and the death penalty suspended in 1965). This first season, then, created the context in which *Cathy Come Home* was produced and then received.

Cathy Come Home: Production Context

Cathy Come Home was drawn from the personal experiences of its author, backed by lengthy and meticulous research. Sandford has commented on how the play came to be written in various interviews and articles, partly as a defence against those critics who charged him with journalistic sloppiness (see Chapter 4). Sandford was married to Nell Dunn, the author of *Up the Junction*, and lived with her in Battersea in the early 1960s (and, like her, was an upper-middle-class incomer). Sandford recalls that a neighbour of theirs was evicted at some point in 1961. 'The family's furniture was thrown out onto the street, and they disappeared, apparently without trace.'[42] Eventually, they were traced to Part III Accommodation, the last form of public housing available to homeless people, and the setting for Cathy's final attempts to keep her family together. 'It was a scene of horror,' he wrote later, 'all the worse for the fact that no one knew about it.' Sandford's description of the conditions he found illustrate his stance as a journalist, committed to helping the people about whom he was researching, and writing from an assumption that his main task was to bring the experience of the socially marginalised before the public gaze.

> Hundreds of families were stacked into an old workhouse. Mothers and children separated from their husbands and fathers, occupying a single

room each or, in some cases, four or five more families shoved into the same room. The toilet facilities were completely inadequate and dysentery was rife. Ambulances called every day, and more than once a day. There was a feeling of complete demoralisation. Husbands were allowed to visit their wives and children only for a couple of hours each night. In the afternoon, even when it was raining, mothers and children were forced out into the streets. They weren't allowed to remain indoors. The reason given for this was that they were meant to be finding accommodation; this was impossible. Obviously, they would hardly be here in these horrible conditions if they hadn't tried to the end of their ability to find accommodation elsewhere.[43]

Sandford's account of his research follows his dramatic method: to use individual experience to access a general, statistically verifiable, truth. Eventually, most women would be evicted from this temporary accommodation, the decision conveyed by 'brutal letter'.

I remember being with one such mother when she received this letter. … She knew what the letter meant. She knew that when she was evicted the children would be taken away from her and put into care. I learned at this time that it was happening to something like twenty-one children per week in the London area alone. I felt that conditions so vile should be brought to the attention of the public.[44]

Sandford's initial response was a journalistic one, to write an exposé in *The Observer* newspaper, which he claimed constituted 'the first ever report in a National newspaper about Britain's homeless'. This was followed by an item on the highly regarded current affairs programme *Panorama*, and several articles in the popular press.[45] He also decided to make a radio documentary with a neighbour, Heather Sutton, who had brought the original case to his attention. The programme, *Homeless Families*, was broadcast in 1961 and consisted of interviews with homeless families intercut with 'what struck me as the somewhat bland and heartless explanations of those who had the job of looking after

23

them'.[46] Sandford managed to record, illegally, in Newington Lodge, one of the most notorious of the Part III reception centres. During this time he befriended a young girl, who risked her own position in the hostel to help them, and who later became a model for Cathy.

The response to *Homeless Families* was, in Sandford's words, 'absolutely nil'.[47] Over the next two years, he continued to write about homelessness for the *People* and *Observer* newspapers, and decided to rework the material as a film for television. He has not been precise about the exact details of the process, but much of the writing seems to have been accomplished over four months between late 1963 and early 1964. The synopsis in the BBC Written Archives is dated 28 January 1965. 'What I conceived was a fairly new idea,' Sandford later wrote, 'half way between drama and documentary, and its newness may have caused a flutter … its time had not yet come.'[48] At one point, the highly regarded Canadian director Ted Kotcheff wanted to direct it and worked with Sandford on the script. 'By the time we finished working on it,' he noted ruefully 'we hoped it would appear as a document in the 1964 General Election, as an indictment of Toryism, but we were unable to find anyone to back it.'[49] The BBC rejected it twice, with both Sydney Newman and Peter Luke, then one of the main producers of The Wednesday Play, expressing reservations. 'One commends his crusading spirit,' Luke wrote, 'but this is documentary stuff … The "Wednesday Play" is not a political platform.'[50] Given the aura of political danger that later surrounded The Wednesday Play this seems spectacularly wrong-headed, but indicates that in its early seasons the series did not have a fixed identity: by the time Garnett found the script, Luke was no longer a producer on The Wednesday Play, and the political weather had changed.

Sandford pushed the manuscript, at this point called *The Abyss*, 'in all sorts of directions'[51] before deciding to turn the material into a novel. The key to the title at this stage is given in the novel, which was eventually completed after the success of the drama and published straight to paperback in 1967 as *Cathy Come Home*. Hinting at a metaphorical purpose that is largely absent from the television film, Cathy says she 'felt they had been living on the edge of an abyss'.[52]

In the latter part of 1965, Sandford received a telephone call from Tony Garnett, who had recently moved from being a story editor to being a drama producer in the rapidly expanding Drama Department, with the power to commission programmes he wanted to make. Garnett told Sandford 'he had found my synopsis at the bottom of the BBC Wednesday Play filing cabinets'[53] and was keen to produce it with Loach as director. Garnett has confirmed Sandford's account.[54] Interestingly, Ken Loach has suggested that he was made aware of the project by a different route at more or less the same time. Loach was introduced to Sandford by his wife, Nell Dunn, with whom he had worked on *Up the Junction*. Sandford 'showed me a two-page outline of *Cathy Come Home*. I remember reading it and being absolutely bowled over by it. Tony and I were very eager to tell the story.'[55] Garnett and Loach already had a working relationship (Garnett had acted in Loach's television debut as a director, *Catherine* (BBC 1964)). Loach had directed several Wednesday Plays, in which Garnett had worked as story editor, notably *Up the Junction*. *The Abyss* was commissioned on 24 January 1966, with a target delivery date of 11 March (it was actually received on 28 March).

A certain mythology has grown around the filming process, in which its makers have emphasised the lengths to which they went to keep the project secret. Noting a degree of circumspection in director and producer, Sandford wrote, sometime after the event, that:

> 'There is one condition,' Tony Garnett had said as we sat in Bertorelli's restaurant in the romantic environment of Shepherds Bush Green, 'attached to our making this film. That you do not speak a word about its content, not a word, until the morning after its transmission. On that condition,' said Tony, 'I'll be happy to send you a contract.' I'd worked previously for newspapers and radio. It hadn't occurred to me that television might be different. Why Garnett's proviso? He explained that there was no way this screenplay would ever be made, let alone transmitted, if the powers that be got to hear of its content.[56]

Sandford's version has been largely substantiated by Garnett.[57]

Until relatively late in the process, *Cathy* was known as *When Cathy Came to Town* (it is referred to as such in the post-production preliminary accounts[58]). By the final budget statement it had become *Cathy Come Home* and was referred to publicly by Newman by its new title in August (see below). Garnett and Sandford resolved that, when asked, they would refer to the film as a 'knock about family comedy'.[59] As Derek Paget has argued, Garnett was particularly keen to keep the true nature of the project hidden from anyone who might be concerned. 'A month before the transmission, Garnett was describing *Cathy* to Gerald Savoury, Head of Plays and Drama, as "a love story" (BBC memo, 26 October 1966) and adopted a strategy of "strategic prevarication".'[60] Garnett's later tactic was to keep any project that was likely to be controversial away from internal scrutiny until after the edition of the *Radio Times*, in which transmission details were published, appeared. If a play was to be withdrawn at this point, he reasoned, it would involve a public row.

However, the BBC did not speak with one voice, and Garnett et al. had their supporters. *Up the Junction* had been made very quickly, and without the full knowledge of either James MacTaggart, its ostensible producer, or Sydney Newman. By the time Garnett commissioned *The Abyss*, he could afford to be a little more open, since he had secured a distinct, if not privileged, position in the Drama Department. In March 1966, Newman wrote a memo to Kenneth Adam, Head of Television, making the case for additional funds for 'thirteen Garnett-type productions' in the Wednesday Play slot, in order to make more drama on film. Noting that Garnett's productions already stood out in the schedules, Newman argued that the increased expenditure could be justified because 'the Garnetts were designed to provide the extra flash of orange every three weeks or so'. Newman linked 'the Garnetts' to the survival of the series itself: 'If the money cannot be found … we may face losing the clear lead we have won in The Wednesday Play field of the single drama.'[61] Newman used Garnett, and *Cathy*, in his defence of controversial material in The Wednesday Play. Announcing the autumn and winter schedules to the press in

August 1966, Newman, in belligerent mood, stated that '[t]here will be at least eight or ten plays on the lines of "Up the Junction" – racy and hard-hitting. Anyone who was moved by that production will be affected by these.' He went on to single out *Cathy Come Home*: 'This will inspire protests,' Mr Newman predicted. 'But they will be about bureaucracy, not the production. This play really grabs hold until the subject yelps.'[62]

Cathy was made very quickly, over a period of about three weeks (5–29 April, 2–6 May and 9–12 May). It was shot mainly on location in Islington, London, and Ladywood in Birmingham, using sound 16mm film. It was also shot in chronological order, a practice which later became Loach's preferred approach. A small amount of filming was done in a studio (on 15 May) under an agreement reached between the BBC and the technicians' unions: an estate agent's office, the court, where an eviction order is granted against Reg, a pub where Reg is drinking with men from the caravan site, for example.[63] The scenes set in Part III hostel accommodation were shot in a real hostel, Newington Lodge, with some of its inhabitants among the cast. Sandford and Garnett were present throughout. As Sandford later observed, the film was 'packed with action',[64] with over a hundred speaking parts. Many of these, and nearly all the non-speaking extras, were recruited from the locations in which the drama was made. 'Vox pop' voiceovers were mainly recorded during the filming process, with some of Sandford's research material added in as well (including interviews recorded for his radio documentary, *Homeless Families*).

Loach later noted that 'The roughness and speed works in favour of the film, but we weren't sure of it at the time.'[65] Made within the time constraints of the studio play, *Cathy* bears signs of stress and strain, with problems solved in situ, Sandford adapting the script along the way. *Cathy Come Home* was the product of both clear vision and improvisation, made to no existing template: to what effect, will be the subject of the next two chapters.

27

2 A Radical Aesthetic

What kind of play/film is *Cathy Come Home* and what is its lineage?
Cathy has been described consistently in terms of its debt to both
dramatic and documentary modes of representation and the tension
between them. Certainly, the insertion of documentary strategies into a
dramatic structure raised questions about the reality status of the film,
for both audiences and critics, and binary oppositions between 'fact'
and 'fiction', 'true' and 'false' and 'real' and 'invented' run though much

of the early critical and popular responses to *Cathy*. That the problems
were predominantly political rather than ontological in nature
heightened their impact. Ultimately, the issue is not one of
categorisation, since any attempt to require the film to conform to
accepted definitions is likely to end in failure. One of the most
interesting, and influential, things about *Cathy* is the way in which it
challenges what is meant by the categories of 'drama' and
'documentary', 'truth' and 'fiction', and how each connects to the social
reality it represents.

It may seem obvious to state this, but no matter how rooted the
story is in Sandford's research, how typical Cathy's situation is of the
homeless, or how socially and politically 'true' the narrative is, it is
nonetheless invented and the dialogue scripted – even if this only begins
to describe *Cathy*'s relationship to social reality. The spine of *Cathy
Come Home* is Cathy's story, and she is clearly the protagonist, in a sense
that is familiar from realist fictions, whose actions and dilemmas provide
the structural heart of the narrative and give the viewer access to other

characters, situations and events, and the social context in which they occur. In having a single protagonist, *Cathy* is in some ways more conventional and less experimental than *Up the Junction*, which has a trio of women at its centre who are protagonists only in the loosest sense. Although Cathy's subjectivity does not control the narrative, there are few scenes in which she is not present. Additionally, the viewer is given access to her thoughts by a voiceover – she is the only character that has this privilege. Sandford was clear from an early stage that he wanted to create a 'dramatised documentary',[66] even if he was not quite certain how the story would be realised. Undoubtedly, *Cathy*'s impact relied on both its content and its choice of methods. Those methods, however, were drawn from different sources, and it is important to obtain a sense of the eclecticism of the acknowledged influences: *Cathy Come Home* is an innovative film, but it did not arrive out of the ether fully formed.

Origins and Influences

One point of reference for the film-makers, critics and audiences was British cinema of the late 1950s and 60s, the films of the 'New Wave' of working-class realism; for example, Jack Clayton's *Room at the Top* (1959, from John Braine's novel), Tony Richardson's *Saturday Night and Sunday Morning* (1960, from Alan Sillitoe's novel) and *A Taste of Honey* (1961, from Shelagh Delaney's play). Like *Cathy*, these films were concerned with the people whose lives were not lived in the glow of affluence, and were often resolutely ordinary, if not socially marginal. Like *Cathy* – and unlike television drama of the same period – New Wave films were shot on location, displaying the socio-geographic settings and creating a 'politics of the visual', to which we will return. Loach has noted that *Cathy*'s makers were consciously 'following in the footsteps' of New Wave cinema, and taking 'the steps towards authenticity a few notches further',[67] especially with regard to acting.

European cinema beyond the UK was also an influence, and both Loach and Garnett have cited the films of the French *nouvelle vague* as important, especially the 1960s films of Jean-Luc Godard, with cinematography by Raoul Coutard. The early films of Milos Forman were a particular point of reference for Loach. As Garnett noted later, 'I'd seen *Breathless* [Godard] and really admired Coutard's work on that, and had a vision of the kind of drama I wanted to do.'[68] Godard/Coutard's use of natural lighting, jump cuts and an observational camera style that evoked a raw, 'on the hoof' style of filming that connoted vérité documentary, helped to create the distinctive filmic 'look' of both *Up the Junction* and *Cathy Come Home*.

Although *Cathy Come Home* is a film that specifically rejects the theatricalised television drama associated with the studio, certain kinds of theatre and stage drama influenced all its creative team, especially the work of the maverick and influential theatre director Joan Littlewood and her company Theatre Workshop, based in the working-class area of London's Stratford East. Littlewood's theatre was rooted firmly in European popular theatre traditions (commedia d'elle' arte, or the high-modernist physicality of the Russian director Vsevelod Meyerhold, for example), as well as British popular culture (music hall, variety). Garnett and Loach were regular visitors to Stratford East in the late 1950s and 1960s, attracted by the clear left-wing politics of the company, the focus on the working class as both theme and putative audience, and the energy and directness of the performance style that combined highly detailed, realistic characterisation with song, dance, comedy and direct address to audience. Like Loach and Garnett, Littlewood frequently used actors who had not been trained by orthodox means (Theatre Workshop had its own exhaustive training programme in the 1950s), or who had not been trained at all. Interestingly, some of the most recognisable actors in British situation comedy of the 1960s and 70s had worked with Littlewood.[69] Several of the cast of *Up the Junction* were ex-members of Theatre Workshop,[70] and Loach had used some of them in other projects.

One of Littlewood's last projects as a director with Theatre Workshop was *Oh What a Lovely War* (1963) an exuberant and episodic account of World War I that combined dramatic and documentary methods – semi-realistic scenes, songs, statistics, projected photographs – framed by the device of an end-of-the-pier Pierrot show. Sandford, as well as Loach and Garnett, saw this production, which presented a model of how dramatic and documentary methods might be combined in the same text. As Sandford commented later, the production had shown him a means by which contextual information might be placed contrapuntally against live-action and fictional scenes, providing a context to it. 'Her use of ticker tape captions going across the stage, carrying crucial general information, underpinning the particular scenes we were being shown, had impressed me,'[71] he noted, and this finds a correspondence in the use of the authoritative voiceover giving statistics and argument in *Cathy Come Home*.

Cathy Come Home uses voiceover of different kinds. Cathy's reflective and subjective voice is juxtaposed with the vox pop of ordinary people, either interviewed for the film or taken from Sandford's earlier researches, which relate to the situations and locations that Cathy and her family find themselves in. There are also voices (mostly male) already mentioned that give statistics and argument, as in a documentary, which contextualise and elaborate upon the experiences that are described in the vox pop or which arise from the dramatic narrative. More pervasively, the entire filmic style of *Cathy Come Home* draws on, and connotes, documentary and current affairs: a restless, single and largely handheld camera (occasionally a tripod was used) that seems to observe, or seek out, social reality rather than cut into it or create it. There is hardly any conventional shot-reverse-shot framing, and the editing strategy relies more on jump cuts and pans than on 'invisible' continuity editing. The cameraman, Tony Imi, had come from documentary and was familiar with the new, lightweight camera technology. The visual 'look' that Loach and Imi strove for came with pre-existing connotations of 'truth', which John Caughie has linked to the 'documentary gaze':

31

> By the documentary gaze I mean the look of the camera which observes the social space and the figures within it ... exploiting the 'objectivity' of the

> camera to constitute its object as 'document'. … the documentary gaze
> depends on systems of mediation (handheld camera, loss of focus,
> awkward framing) so visible as to become immediate, apparently
> unrehearsed, and hence authentic.[72]

This contrasted sharply with the dominant practices of television drama production, which were wedded to the formality of the two-camera studio shoot.

Looking at some of the public and in-house BBC responses to *Cathy*, one could be forgiven for thinking that the idea of dramatising documentary research was entirely new and inherently disreputable (see Chapter 4). However, there was an established tradition of dramatised documentaries (using documentary in the loosest sense to embrace the non-fictional in early television). As Scannell has written, the dramatised documentary was 'one of the first specifically televisual forms of production'[73] and was studio-based and live:

> it was scripted, rehearsed and used actors; it had filmed inserts for
> continuity and location sequences. Its subject matter was drawn from
> current (but not immediately topical) issues of social concern. … Among
> the issues handled by the dramatized documentary between 1946 and
> 1956 were delinquency, youth, marriage, old age, runaway children,
> prostitution.[74]

The titles of these dramatised documentaries give an idea of the topics covered: *Magistrates Court* (1948), *Missing from Home* (1955), *Report on Women* (1954) and *The Tearaway* (1956). Dramatisation of documentary material was necessary in order to overcome the technical limitations of studio-bound, live transmission.

A later and more directly influential practice, although it does not involve the dramatic, would be the documentary/current affairs films of Dennis Mitchell, who used a lightweight, silent 16mm camera and portable sound equipment to make evocative portraits of working-class communities. As Jamie Sexton has observed, in *Morning in the*

Streets (BBC 1959), for example, 'a working-class milieu is evoked through an accumulation of carefully composed images, whilst working-class voices express their views on various aspects of life'.[75] The montage of voice and image in Mitchell's films prefigures one strategy of *Cathy Come Home*. The key issue here is that Mitchell used *film* and the development of documentary/drama hybrids after this point is bound up with that of 16mm film technology. Noting the initial institutional resistance to the 'inferior' grainy quality of the 16mm image, Sexton has charted the ways in which lightweight 16mm cameras, with synchronised sound, were gradually adopted by UK documentary film-makers (especially the ground-breaking *World in Action* current affairs series), influenced by the new wave of 'direct cinema' documentaries emanating from the USA.[76] However, *Cathy Come Home*'s combination of different storytelling modes goes some way beyond the available models for 'dramatised documentaries' or documentary drama.

In order to be allowed to use film on *Up the Junction*, Garnett had to convince Michael Peacock, Controller of BBC1, the BBC studios at Ealing (the film-making department within the Corporation) and Sydney Newman, Garnett's immediate boss. This was essentially a rerun of the arguments that documentary and features film-makers had had with their respective bosses, with the added dimension that the resistance to film was underpinned by an aesthetic ideology for drama that favoured 'liveness' and the studio. The pressure to remain in the studio was intense, especially as the BBC had invested in new studios at the White City, anticipating the increase in drama production with the arrival of BBC2 in 1964. Newman, with his background in commercial film production, did not need much persuading, but Peacock was extremely reluctant, arguing that the Drama Department should produce 'A plays rather than B movies'.[77] He agreed to it as a one-off experiment, but after the success of both *Up the Junction* and *Cathy Come Home*, the argument against film had lost some its political and aesthetic weight. Film, especially the highly flexible technology of synchronised 16mm, had opened up new possibilities.

Cathy Come Home: Narrative Structure

The narrative of *Cathy Come Home* is complex in its detail, and is dense and episodic; however, it has an overarching structure that is easy to summarise. John Corner[78] has argued that it is most easily understood as having three main sections. The first concerns Cathy's arrival in London, where she meets and marries Reg, moves into a flat with him and becomes pregnant. It concludes with Reg's accident, which means that the new family must look for somewhere else to live. The second section begins to trace their descent through the housing system, as their family increases to three children. Section three begins with Cathy's arrival in a hostel for the homeless, at which point the disintegration of the family enters its final stages. For Sandford, the story, which corresponds to a classic naturalist dramatic structure of a journey into misery, is one of a family falling apart as it passes through the housing system, and its structure emphasises this. It is worth keeping this overall trajectory in mind when considering the narrative in a more detailed way.

In a film as layered and dense as *Cathy*, a detailed account of the narrative is difficult and can be accomplished in different ways, depending on the aim of one's analysis; and any description that focuses on narrative events inevitably distorts the viewing experience of a film that is structured through a montage of voice and image. Here, the major sequences and scenes will be detailed, and a summary of the main action provided, indicating where voiceover occurs. An account of the significance of these, along with the film's visual and performative structures and its use of time and place, comes later.

Arrival

The first sequence of the film concerns Cathy's arrival in London. It begins with a head-and-shoulders close-up of Cathy (Carol White) in bright sunshine waiting by the side of the road. '500 Miles' by Sonny and Cher is played non-diegetically on the soundtrack. The title credit

rolls, followed by 'A Story by Jeremy Sandford'. Cathy is given a lift into
London, her journey narrated in retrospect by her as a voiceover from a
presumed present, as if to explain the glimpses of the city we are
witnessing from the lorry window.

Courtship

At just over a minute into the film, Reg (Ray Brooks) appears (although
we do not see them meet) and a short sequence of courtship follows.
This is in the form of a montage of episodes from a longer narrative: a
walk along the side of a canal, in which the lovers kiss (filtered
romantically by leaves); free-wheeling conversations, one framed in a
doorway and another on a park bench; their first row on leaving a
cinema; Reg explaining his job to Cathy as he gives her a lift in his van.
Reg's proposal of marriage, when it comes, is downbeat and
conversational, and is accepted in similar terms. Reg and Cathy have
climbed the scaffolding surrounding a building near where Reg works,

and the scene affords one of the few glimpses of the landscape of London from above street level.

The wedding

There is a sudden jump from the relative quietness of the proposal scene to the noise and bustle of Reg and Cathy's wedding party. The first image, in case we should be in doubt, is of Cathy in her wedding dress. The party, like the pub scenes in *Up the Junction*, is shot with a roving, observational camera, eavesdropping on stories that are picked out of a noisy soundtrack that threatens to drown out the foregrounded conversations. Reg's mum (Winifred Dennis) and grandad (Wally Patch) are picked out of the crowd for our attention. This sequence concludes with Reg and Cathy laughing loudly, and is followed by an abrupt transition to a close-up of Grandad, now at home. There are only two voices to be heard, those of Reg's mum and a welfare officer (Gabrielle Hamilton). The dialogue establishes that the flat is

37

overcrowded, and that Grandad is to go to a home. As the news is given, the camera zooms slowly from mid-shot into close-up on Grandad's face. He is crying.

The good times

Another abrupt transition takes the viewer to Cathy and Reg's new flat and the sequence that follows establishes that they are in a carefree and relatively affluent period of their lives, although the dialogue establishes Cathy's anxiety ('Do you think we're overstepping?'). This sequence ends with Cathy discovering she is pregnant. Her resigned acceptance is narrated over a (real) ante-natal class. Cathy visits an estate agent (Geoffrey Palmer), in the first of several meetings with officials of different kinds that punctuate the drama, and discovers that people in her and Reg's position stand little chance of affording to buy a property of their own.

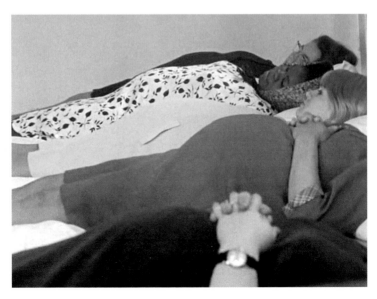

The good times end

Another abrupt transition confronts the viewer with the event that is to
precipitate the disasters that follow: Reg is injured in a van accident,
which leaves him unable to work for a time. The crash is represented by
a montage of close-ups and sound effects, and as he is removed from the
wreckage on a stretcher, a voiceover conversation between Reg and his
boss, from a presumed near future, reveals that there will be no
compensation. The details of Reg's injuries are never fully explained, but
this disruption to their way of life results in Cathy and Reg resolving to
leave their flat. Two structural devices enter the narrative at this point:
the first is that of Cathy walking the streets, knocking on doors in an
unsuccessful attempt to find a home – it is a motif that will repeated,
mostly with Reg and their expanding family in tow, throughout the film:
the second is a documentary-style voiceover conveying information
about the housing crisis, of which Cathy and Reg's dilemma is an
example. This discourse of authority will become one of the main forms

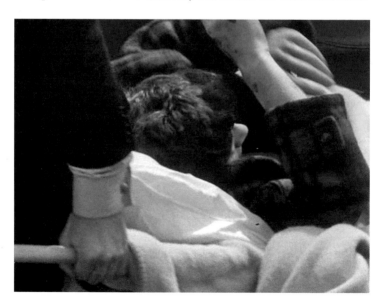

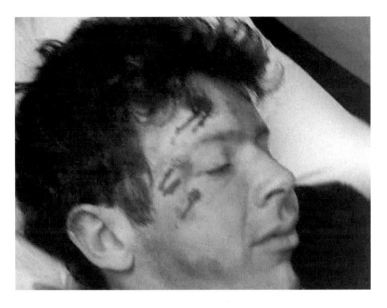

of factual address in the film. The sequence ends with the couple, having been informed by a property agent of what it will cost to rent a new flat, acknowledging defeat and going to live with Reg's mum. Cathy's voiceover recognises that this was 'goodbye to freedom'. The sequence ends with a blank screen.

The downward spiral: living with the Wards

Over the next few months, Reg, Cathy and the first child, Sean (Mylene in the published script) live with Reg's mum and his brother and sister in a flat that the viewer already knows to be overcrowded. This sequence, especially its opening scenes, has been analysed in some depth by both Corner (1996) and Leigh (2002), since it provides a particularly good example of the way that the film combines fictional and documentary-style narrative techniques, and maps the Ward family's personal story against a wider social and cultural experience. A montage of visual images from the block of tenement flats (Islington, London) is

42

juxtaposed with documentary-style voiceover that consists mainly of comments by residents about their living conditions. This is the first appearance of another discourse, that of ordinary people (vox pop), which will be heard throughout the rest of the film as the Wards progress through the housing system. Alongside these sequences, and interspersed with them, are a series of scenes within the home, which show the domestic life of the extended Ward family. Although good-humoured at first, tensions soon arise, and their short stay comes to an abrupt end when Cathy and Reg's mum fall out.

The downward spiral: Birmingham

Cathy's narrative voiceover informs us that she and Reg decided to try a new city, at about the same time as their second child (Stevie)

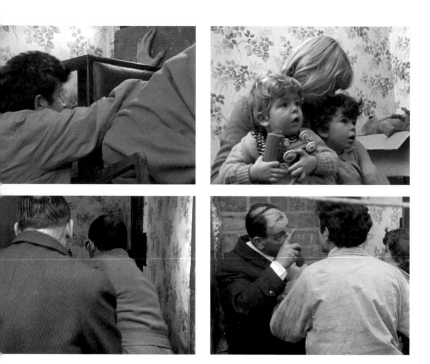

arrives, and the action moves to Birmingham. Reg obtains a new job, and the family finds a degree of stability, if not security. Vox pop voiceovers give a variety of perspectives on housing conditions – they are living in what is deemed to be a 'rough place' – and community life. Reg continues to be troubled with ill-health, and cannot find regular work, with the result that the family falls behind with their rent. Nevertheless, as Cathy's voiceover informs us, the family feel 'settled'. This precarious existence ends with the death of their landlady, Mrs Alley (Phyllis Hickson). A distant nephew claims the property for his family and takes the Wards to court for rent arrears. In front of the magistrate, Reg is unconvincing (he has lost the rent book), with the result that an eviction order is granted. A new cycle of fruitless street-walking and house hunting begins, during which Cathy's voiceover makes clear that it is the children that are the main

obstacle to finding a house. The family, increasingly
uncomprehending of the situation that is engulfing them, prepare to
defend their home. There follows a meeting with a sympathetic
housing official who puts them on a waiting list for the new Smithson
Estate of council houses, but can offer no immediate solution to their
problems. A housing official visits and condemns the property as unfit
to live in, but they are evicted before any action he can take comes
into effect. The eviction, which is accompanied by a montage of
voiceovers outlining the wider context, is dramatised in brutal detail
(Reg makes a futile attempt to board up the front door) and watched
by the neighbourhood. The Ward family, which now includes three
children, are on the streets again. This sequence concludes at just
under half way through the narrative.

The downward spiral: the caravan

Cathy, Reg and family move to a caravan site, where they have bought
their own small and dishevelled caravan (quite where this is is never
fully explained). Life on the site is revealed in ways that are now
becoming familiar: a montage of short scenes, mostly encounters with
fellow caravan-dwellers and children playing, are juxtaposed with
voiceover commentary, mostly of residents. Cathy continues to provide
an interpretative framework for both visual and aural discourses,
explaining that, although conditions are harsh, there is a kind of peace
to be found: 'It's as if we'd sunk out of the race.' However, society has
not forgotten them, and events rapidly move beyond their control. At a
meeting of ratepayers from a nearby housing estate, the caravan-
dwellers are denounced as 'scroungers' (it is one of the very few scenes in
the drama that does not involve Cathy or Reg) and confrontation is
inevitable. A caravan is attacked and set on fire, resulting in the death of
two children. The narrative context for this is provided by the voiceover
of a surviving child addressing a coroner's court, which is played over a
montage of the burning caravan and the futile attempts to rescue those
trapped within it. The predictable result is that the site, now on the

45

authorities' radar, is closed and the Wards' caravan is towed away. They
are repeatedly harassed and moved on by the police, and are forced to
sell the caravan.

The downward spiral: last stages

A new stage in the cycle begins, and in rapid succession the family
are cheated out of a house (Reg pays a deposit to a 'man in a pub', only
to find it boarded up prior to demolition); attempt, unsuccessfully, to
rent a narrow boat on an inland waterway; stay briefly in a derelict
house, which has no windows or proper roof; and sleep overnight under
a makeshift tent. It is clear that the children's health is deteriorating. In a
last gesture against fate, the family enjoy a drink and crisps in a pub and
resolve to go to a hostel for the homeless.

The downward spiral: the hostel system

This final stage in the family's disintegration, which charts their encounter with statutory housing services, begins just under three-quarters of the way through the narrative and probably has the most potent emotional effect on the viewer. The Ward family are referred to Cumbermere Lodge, and their first encounter with it is an interview with an official, in which the terms on which hostel accommodation is offered is explained: it is 'emergency accommodation' offered to people on a temporary basis while they secure permanent housing for themselves. Men are not allowed to stay ('they tear up the sheets') and Reg has to leave. As Cathy and the children walk resignedly into the depths of the building, climbing seemingly endless flights of stairs, a montage of voiceovers of residents and officials provide experiences that

parallel, generalise and comment on Cathy's. Later that first night, Reg breaks into the hostel and visits Cathy. In one of the few moments of emotional release in the film, Cathy breaks down and cries and the couple make love.

Life in the hostel is sketched out in telling details – food that has to be queued for, and is inedible when it arrives, broken cups that harbour disease, recurrent infections and illnesses, violent emotional arguments between desperate people over nothing. The pressures on Cathy and Reg become evident, and they argue over the little money that Reg's meagre wage provides. The children become ill, and Cathy asks Reg's mum to look after the eldest child for a time. In a new meeting with officials, Cathy is reminded of the temporary nature of the accommodation and that she and the children must move to a Part III hostel. In a particularly bitter blow, Cathy learns that the family have lost their place on the waiting list for the Smithson Estate, having left the area. She loses her temper and is pacified.

Cathy and her children then enter the Part III hostel, named, in a cruel echo of bourgeois gentility, Holm Lea. We see it first as if through her eyes, and her concern is echoed in the voiceover testimonies of the women that we hear on the soundtrack. It is clear that everyone in this hostel has a story similar to Cathy's, and the women constitute a supportive group. Reg announces that he will go to Liverpool in search of work, and Cathy supports his choice. It is, however, the last time we see him; he ceases to pay the rent, we later learn. Left alone, Cathy does not succumb to the indignities of hostel life easily. She fights with a nurse after the death of a baby in the hostel. In an echo of the real-life Cathy, whom Sandford befriended, she apparently talks to the press about hostel conditions (although this is

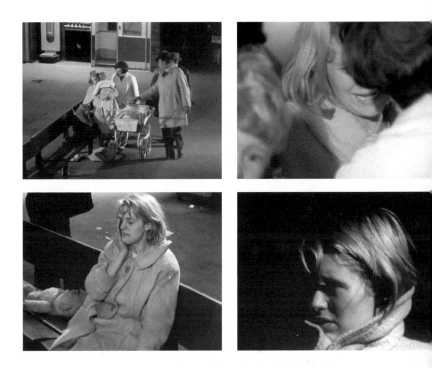

never confirmed nor denied by her). After a final, ill-tempered meeting
with officials, she receives a letter confirming that she will be required
to leave the hostel.

The end of the road

There is now a strong sense of events escalating, as Cathy is warned 'not
to make a fuss when the time comes'. She packs her bag, walks the
streets once more and arrives at Liverpool Street Station, in a montage
that is linked by Cathy's voiceover narrative (lasting just under three
minutes). In this final sequence, which probably did more than any
other to anchor the emotional impact of the film, welfare officials
forcibly remove Cathy's children from her. She is left alone on the
station, sobbing. The film concludes, in a book-end manner, with a shot

of Cathy behind the credits in close-up, presumably waiting for a lift out of London, which refers to the opening image. '500 Miles' once again play over the sound of traffic. This time, however, it is dark and the tones are muted. There are three concluding captions that play over the still of Cathy's face:

1. All the events in this film took place in Britain within the last eighteen months.
2. 4,000 children are separated from their parents and taken into care each year because their parents are homeless.
3. West Germany has built twice as many houses as Britain since the War.

Narrative Stance: Naturalism and Objectivity

Loach's films are often called naturalist, although the terminology is inexact. It is certainly not the kind of naturalism that Troy Kennedy Martin castigated in his manifesto for a new television drama in *Encore*[79] (discussed in Chapter 1). Nor is it used in the sense that it often is in the context of post-war stage drama – that is, as shorthand for the scenic literalism of 'box sets'. Naturalism, in some of its colloquial uses, is relevant, however. The desire to reproduce the observable forms of social reality in all its rich visual and aural detail, for example, in a visual style that connotes 'truth', represents documentary-drama and social realism in its naturalist form.

Naturalism also equates to the suppression of symbolism and metaphor, in favour of metonymy and description. In this sense, Cathy acts not as a symbol of a social problem, but rather as a metonym for it, a particular instance of a general predicament. *Cathy* works hard to eradicate symbolism of any kind, since symbolism and metaphor often take attention away from the social reality that is being represented and direct it towards the workings of the narrative; it is a central aim of naturalism, which *Cathy* undoubtedly shares,

52

to focus attention on the issues raised by the story rather than the telling itself.

Some of the changes made to *Cathy*'s script once Loach and Garnett had been brought into the process give an insight into Loach's approach and to the difference that a naturalist approach could make. Sandford's treatment for *The Abyss* included a scene in which Reg, Cathy and the children blow 'their last fiver on a night in a Grand Hotel, where they dine as the band plays'.[80] This might well have made for a dramatically effective scene, but the symbolic contrasts it suggests would have been at odds with the naturalism of the rest of the film and with the logic of how a family in this situation might plausibly behave (and Cathy and Reg would have drawn criticism for the profligacy of spending so much at a time of crisis). In the struggle between credibility and dramatic effect, naturalism dictates that the former must always win. What remains is a much more prosaic short scene in a pub garden in which the family eat crisps and drink beer and lemonade and the decision is made to enter the hostel system.

Deborah Knight has argued persuasively that Loach should be considered a naturalist, in a more complex and historical sense[81] and the argument applies to *Cathy Come Home*. Naturalism in this usage is a manifestation of a philosophical and aesthetic position linked to the natural sciences. Naturalists were, and are, concerned primarily with the determining power of the environment on human behaviour, with how social, genetic, economic and political factors shape the choices and possibilities of their characters' lives. Naturalist texts are, in the tradition of the French novelist Emile Zola, a form of experiment, in which a social situation is set up and its determinist logic pursued to a conclusion. Typically, characters in naturalist novels/plays/films start bad and end up worse and the disintegration of Cathy and Reg's family can be seen as a variation on that pattern (they at least know happiness). It is difficult at times to be sure when a conviction that external, environmental forces shape individual lives becomes a pessimism that nothing can be done to resist those forces, and *Cathy* has been charged with falling into a grim fatalism. However, it is one of the functions of the voice of authority on the film's soundtrack to suggest that there *is* something that can be done to alleviate the Ward family's situation – build more houses.

What *Cathy* has in common with Zolaesque naturalism is that it confronts its characters with forces that they cannot control, offering 'a perspective from which to understand the social mechanisms that perpetuate ... irreconcilable conflicts between what characters desire and what they can achieve'.[82] This leads to a form of objectivity, where 'the point of these narratives is not to present and resolve a problem, but to make plain the nature of the problem and its consequences in terms of characters' lives'.[83] The term 'objectivity' is a difficult one to use in postmodern times, and should not be taken to mean omniscience. Objectivity implies a narrative that creates a distance from the situation it portrays, standing outside events and looking in, as it were. This defines the dominant narrative stance in *Cathy Come Home* and has consequences for the ways in which the viewer is addressed (although, like any film, a moment-by-moment analysis suggests that other narrative positions are also present).

There is one sense in which the narrative of *Cathy Come Home* is not 'third person'. Cathy has a voiceover, which creates a viewpoint on some of the events that the film describes, and underscores her position as protagonist of the narrative. Its function is complex. Derek Paget has argued that Cathy's voice gives the narrative a 'classical' shape, which he relates to Loach's influence on Sandford's reworking of the early part of the story. The opening section uses Cathy's dual perspective – a voice looking back on her youthful self – to establish a premise that the film then proceeds to explore. It is described thus in the screenplay:

> A YOUNG GIRL stands by the entrance to the motorway, waiting for a lift.
>
> She shifts from one foot to the other, walks a little, impeded by her 'smart' shoes, turns round as lorries or cars pass.
>
> She's evidently been left here by another car that brought her this far. She's young, pretty, and with an air of excitement about her; freed at last

from ties to her family, heart-whole, at the age of consent, but
unconsenting as yet, exultant yet shy. She carries a change of clothes,
shoes, etc. in a parcel.

With a hiss of its steam brakes a lorry draws to a stop ahead of her.[84]

This stands as a judgment of Cathy at this stage of her journey
and is almost identical to the opening of the novel. It is translated by
Loach into a short, steady, head-and-shoulders close-up. As Cathy
climbs into the lorry, we hear her voiceover for the first time: 'Well, I
was a bit fed up … didn't seem to be much there for me … you know
how these little towns are … *one* coffee bar … it was closed on a
Sunday.'[85] The clear import of this device is that the main action of the
drama occurs in the past tense, a 'then', and that Cathy's commentary is
from a narrative present, a 'now'. It is an indication of the deliberate
temporal imprecision of the film as a whole that the viewer is not
informed of exactly how much time separates 'then' from 'now'. The
device, as John Corner notes, functions partly 'as a "speech" version of
the first-person novelistic narration'[86] but this does not fully account for
the way that Cathy addresses us, since she is not simply describing what
we see: we have evidence for it that is independent of her comments.
Significantly, the film removed several purely 'informational' voiceovers
from Sandford's text (the published screenplay), in which Cathy controls
the viewer's progress between one scene and the next, and this
undermines the sense of Cathy as our sole point of view on the events of
the narrative.

Much of the time, Cathy in the present seems to be responding
to events that we witness, reflecting and commenting rather than
introducing us to them, or controlling our access to them. She is at the
viewer's elbow, looking on at the narrative rather than standing between
viewer and dramatic incident. As Corner observes, 'the discursive
alignment is not dissimilar from someone talking about the images in a
photograph album, the pages of which are being turned by another
person'.[87] It also suggests an intimacy that acknowledges the domestic
context in which the film is being experienced by the viewer. Cathy is, as

it were, in the living room with us, rather than addressing us from the screen of a darkened auditorium. The effect is sometimes a curious one, and Cathy's commentary easily blurs into the 'now' of the narrative, striking the viewer 'with the force of present consciousness',[88] while still being markedly different in kind to the other, unidentified voices that we hear.

The question of how audiences might be helped to resolve the problem that *Cathy* poses may also be considered in relation to the film's debt to melodrama. Walker and Leigh have both argued that *Cathy Come Home* is essentially a 'melodrama of protest',[89] which Walker links to the classics of cinema history, Eisenstein's *Battleship Potemkin* (1925) and D. W. Griffith's *Intolerance* (1916) and *Birth of a Nation* (1915). More contemporary, though post-*Cathy* examples are the US television series *Roots* (ABC 1977), which dealt with black history through the prism of a family, and Loach and Garnett's *Days of Hope*, which dealt with British working-class history from World War I to the General Strike of 1926. Like *Cathy*, *Days of Hope* was a story of defeat, although it was the defeat of an entire political movement that was at stake here, and, Walker argues, represented an 'Anglicisation' of the form.[90] Walker uses melodrama in the sense that it has come to be used in film studies, as both a historical form (although not bound to its origins in nineteenth-century theatre) and a certain kind of character and narrative structure available at any historical period. Melodrama is not being used here as a generally derogatory critical term, and requires one to put aside the association with narrative and performative excess and see the connections between melodrama and naturalism. The protagonists of melodrama, as Walker reminds us, are essentially 'undivided, "whole", free from the tensions of choosing between conflicting loyalties, imperatives or desires. The forces with which such a hero must grapple are external: oppression, corruption, villainy in general, "natural" disasters.'[91] Cathy is a heroine in this mould in that the drama is not much interested in her internal dilemmas (or, indeed, anyone's internal dilemmas).

There is little conventional character development in *Cathy Come Home*, and the forces with which Cathy must contend lie

57

outside of her. In this sense, the film does not follow a conventional narrative pattern and there is no indication of how, and if, her experiences have changed her. This owes as much to Sandford's insistence on her status as Everywoman as it does to the conventions of melodrama. She is presented as an innocent who finds herself in difficult circumstances through no fault of her own (although some critics were keen to blame her for having three children). Her plight invites recognition and sympathy: anyone could find themselves in such a situation, if the circumstances were so placed. Cathy is also very much in the naturalist mode in that she is resolutely 'ordinary' and anti-heroic, an example of a working-class woman struggling to survive in difficult circumstances.

The protagonist of a melodrama of protest exists within a narrative, that 'sets out to attack established ideology, to expose injustice, to champion reform or even to incite revolution'[92] and does so largely by arousing emotion by dramatising the problem in terms of its effects on a family. One need not be engaged in heroic, or obviously 'political', activities in order for the argument to apply, and it is a part of the political project of naturalism that the structural defects and governing ideologies of society may be accessed through the lives of unexceptional characters. It is essentially through the characters' failure to change, or exert control over, the circumstances of the narrative that the power of the drama lies: it is hard to imagine that *Cathy* would have had the same emotional or political impact if the Ward family had managed to find a house and stayed together. Hence, melodramas of protest, like naturalist dramas, end, inevitably, in defeat.[93] The defeat is presented as a logical outcome of the naturalist 'experiment' that the narrative has put in place; it is for the audience, and not the text, to determine what happens next. *Cathy Come Home* demands that the housing crisis be addressed, and the solution to build more houses is inescapable. However, in choosing to end the story at the point of maximum drama, with Cathy's children wrenched from her grasp as in a classical melodrama, Sandford and Loach have avoided tracing the precise ways in which the situation might be made different; there is no route map for how we get from where we are to where we want to be. To refuse to provide such a way forward is not necessarily a problem, however; in naturalism, finding solutions belongs to the realm of politics, not television, and the solution is left to the audience.

Depersonalisation, Generalisation and Contextualisation

Another sense in which *Cathy Come Home* adopts a certain objectivity towards its characters lies in what one might call a process of de-personalisation, or generalisation, and this is linked to what Sandford termed 'contextualisation'. Sandford described *Cathy Come Home* as the story of an 'Everyman' (or woman) and the play as a form of morality tale, echoing the medieval morality plays, in which the evil confronted is in the form of an uncaring welfare state.

> I tried to quintessentialize [the subject] dramatically. Cathy is Everywoman, Everymother, a woman who just thinks that children are God's gift, coming up against state machinery, which results in the decimation of her family. Her natural instincts and desires are destroyed by the institutionalized violence of a state.[94]

There is a systematic lack of detail concerning Cathy's background in the film, and a consequent absence of psychological individuality and motivation at times, which was intended to make Cathy open to identification. 'I didn't want Cathy to have too strong a character,' Sandford noted, meaning that she should not appear too individualised, 'I wanted her to be the kind of person the maximum number of people could identify with.'[95]

This conscious refusal to be specific about Cathy's history is echoed elsewhere in the narrative, and there is a systematic avoidance in the film of formal exposition and explanation. Viewers are moved quickly into the story, given very little of the kind of detail that a more

conventional 'classical' narrative might take for granted – Cathy and
Reg's first meeting, for example, or a smoother, fuller account of their
courtship. The strategy is more noticeable when the film is placed
alongside the screenplay and subsequent novelisation. In both
screenplay and novel, for example, Reg has a scene in the hospital after
his accident in which he is told his career as a long-distance driver is over
(in the screenplay, Cathy is given informational voiceovers, the main
purpose of which is to provide a transition from one scene to another,
but these are omitted from the film).

Additionally, we spend a lot of time with Cathy and Reg but it
is remarkable how little we discover about them – their personal
histories, in particular. *Cathy Come Home*, the novelisation, contains a
lot more by way of background information than either screenplay or
film. The reader learns that Cathy came to London from somewhere in
the Midlands; that she was about to be laid off when she got pregnant
('they're laying us all off anyway, at Christmas. They got these new
machines, they won't need us no more'[96]); and that she had been taken
into care and placed 'in an institution' for two years when she was six
years old because 'her Mum and Dad hadn't been able ever to see eye to
eye in those days'.[97] The experience left her determined 'to get for herself
a better life than her Mum had'.[98] The novel also gives the reader more
insight into Cathy's subjective response to events, tracing her thoughts
and emotions in more detail than either film or screenplay – although
access to her interior life is still fairly limited.

The stripping away of this kind of psychological and
biographical information is one instance of a deeper intention that runs
through each iteration of Cathy's story, which is to find ways of relating
the particular to the general, the personal story to the social one. For
Cathy Come Home to work politically, it needs to convince its audience
of the 'truth', or typicality, of Cathy's story. At one level, all naturalist –
and not just naturalist – narratives do this, with their central characters
'standing in' metonymically for others in a similar predicament.
Contemporary press reviews responded to this, sometimes challenging
the typicality of Cathy's situation. As Sandford, who resented and

contested the accusations at every opportunity, later wrote, 'people tell me that all the things that happened to Cathy could not have happened to one girl. ... A newspaper working under my guidance, once sent out fifty reporters to seek out Britain's "true-life Cathys". The stories they sent back were, without exception, far more complicated than Cathy's.'[99]

Cathy Come Home goes to considerable lengths to establish the typicality of Cathy's story and to depict a social as well as an individual problem, not least through the incorporation of the kind of documentary elements already noted, in particular the voiceovers. Sandford, a journalist by training it should be remembered, was clear about the purpose of this strategy, seeing it as a means of providing 'contextualisation' of Cathy's story for a political purpose.

Contextualisation is presenting our viewers with two things at once, in counterpoint. There is the particular story of Cathy and the series of misfortunes that led to her so tragically losing her children. This is presented in traditional film makers' story telling mode with a succession of scenes and synch dialogue.

Running simultaneously is the contextualisation. This uses the voices of real people caught in the same predicament, the sort of material one would use in a documentary. Most of the actuality voices used as wildtrack or voiceovers in 'Cathy' had been originally used in BBC radio documentaries that I had recorded and made myself.

These voices underpin and endorse the particular story of 'Cathy' with generalised comments. ...

The contextualisation also used statistics spoken and on screen, the voices of professional type people commenting, and even the voice of Cathy herself telling her story and musing on her predicament.

The effect of all these voices used as voice overs is to widen out the unique picture of Cathy's predicament and put it in the context of all these other British people who were suffering the effects of a man-made housing famine, all those people who were suffering in hostels for the homeless, needlessly having their children taken from them.[100]

61

The 'widening out' that Sandford refers to is linked to the film's distinctive mode of address, which Corner (1996) and Leigh (2002) refer to as a combination of 'story' and 'report'. The former refers to the dramatic narrative of Cathy and her family; the latter relates to the documentary discourses the film uses in general, and involves more than the contextualising testimonies. However, in the hierarchy of discourses, it is these voices that carry the most weight as authentication. The technique of contextualisation is most apparent at moments of narrative transition, mapping the Ward family's descent through the housing system: when Cathy and Reg go to live with Reg's mum, for example, or when the family leave London for Birmingham, or move to a caravan following their eviction. At these points, voiceovers of all kinds are intercut with dialogue, sometimes replacing it.

A viewer could imagine what the effect of the removal of these techniques might be on the way *Cathy*'s story is told and how the viewer relates to it. Although there is little of the conventional rhetoric of the dramatic look in the film, the effect of the documentary gaze, combined with the strategies of depersonalisation and generalisation, might well render Cathy, her family and her class collectively passive, inert objects of the camera's unswerving eye. *Cathy*'s use of contextualising techniques, however, makes the working class the subject of the drama, and not simply part of the backdrop. The personal testimonies stand as historical document as well as narrative device, while the 'voices of authority' place both these and the story elements in a sociological context. Through the voices of individuals, a collective experience is sketched out and offered against the dominant discourses of public debate.

Cathy Come Home, in its film incarnation more than any of the others, opts for spatial-temporal generalisation: that is, it refuses to be specific about where or when the narrative occurs, which might seem surprising for a film that is so determined to speak to its immediate social and political context. Indeed, the film is relatively clear about its location in historical time and place: visually, the pulling down of traditional, urban, back-to-back terraces and the suggestion of a property boom based on home ownership are present in the film. Narrative chronology and location, however, are much less precisely defined, and it is often difficult to be sure exactly where and when different events are taking place. The first sequence establishes Cathy's arrival in London, although this is by inference and through what we see as much as through the voiceover (there is no dialogue). When Cathy and her family leave Reg's mum's house to try their luck in another town they move to Birmingham, but, once again, the precise location is not confirmed by anything in the dialogue or voiceover. Similarly, when the family are evicted from their condemned house in Birmingham, they move back south, presumably to London (where they remain), to live in a caravan – again, the viewer is not told this directly at any point. The film, which borrows heavily from the rhetoric of documentary in other respects, avoids on-screen captions that might indicate where Cathy's journey has taken her (and us). Information about place is contained visually, of course, but not through identifiable markers of location; unless one has specific local knowledge, it is often hard to be clear about the distinctions between poor, working-class areas of London and Birmingham – but then this is part of the politics of the film. *Cathy* is about a national issue. Loach argued that the move to Birmingham, which brought problems to a shooting schedule already under pressure, was necessary because 'we didn't want it to be seen as only a London problem'.[101]

63

There is a similar difficulty about being sure of the duration of the narrative. One of the captions over the final credits runs 'All the events in this film happened in Britain in the last eighteen months,' but this is most likely a statement about the relevance of the research, rather than a summary of the narrative chronology. Narrative time is indicated in the script and novel more clearly, but only relatively so. The screenplay measures time partly in relation to Cathy and Reg's wedding. Shortly before Cathy and Reg decide to leave his mum's overcrowded flat, we are told that it is now 'Seventeen months after the Wedding'.[102] At the end of that scene, the action switches to Birmingham, and we are informed that it is now 'Three years after Wedding',[103] but it is hard to map that onto our experience of the film, which seems to develop at a somewhat slower pace at this point (the figure of three years relates more closely to the point in the narrative where Cathy and Reg are about to be evicted). Time is measured mostly by the arrival of Cathy and Reg's three children, and their subsequent growing up. Although their ages are not mentioned, it is likely, though not certain, that the narrative takes place over a little more than five years (factoring in the amount of time devoted to Cathy's story before the children arrive).

Taken together, spatial-temporal generalisation, the removal of biographical information and the avoidance of exposition, suggest that the formal strategies of *Cathy Come Home* are more complex and varied than the term documentary-drama normally allows: without ever ceasing to be naturalist, in the sense defined above, *Cathy* is more than merely 'naturalistic'. The focus on a single protagonist in *Cathy* may help to keep the documentary elements in order, but there is still an openness to the narrative that offers different ways of accessing the film's meanings. Sandford has commented on the density of the *Cathy*'s storytelling, arguing that its montage structure meant that it was intended 'more contrapuntally' than orthodox narratives, with the result that 'people remember different things about the film', indicating that 'the viewer subconsciously has to make a selection'.[104]

John Caughie has argued convincingly that the strategies of montage used in both *Up the Junction* and *Cathy Come Home* connect them to British modernist documentary practices from the 1920s and 1930s, a tradition that is represented in the films of Dennis Mitchell and which 'stretches back through Free Cinema, Humphrey Jennings, *Night Mail*, to Cavalcanti and the experimentation with sound/image juxtapositions which he brought to the Documentary movement from his experience of surrealist cinema in France'.[105] This tradition also links to European modernism through Eisenstein's writings on sound and image.

The kind of modernism Caughie traces is one that privileges montage over narrative continuity, is multi-vocal and contains an unstable relationship between sound and image, and which is open to different readings that might well disorient the viewer. This form of

modernism is also connected, in another direction, to the theory and
practice of the German writer, theorist, director and poet Berthold
Brecht, who cast a long shadow across British culture in the second half
of the twentieth century. Both Garnett and Loach have acknowledged the
debt, and Leigh has argued that 'all Loach's work of the mid-1960s
shows the equivocal influence of Brechtian techniques'.[106] The use of the
word 'equivocal' is telling and accurate, suggesting that Loach's interest
in Brecht, like that of his peers, was often pragmatic and filtered through
other preoccupations and influences. Garnett said that Brecht was one of
the main reasons why he and Loach were interested in documentary
technique in a dramatic context. In an interview with Lez Cooke, Garnett
commented on the way that Brecht demonstrated a means of holding
emotion and analysis in tension and of disrupting viewer expectations.
His comments refer to *Up the Junction*, but also apply to *Cathy*.

> it wasn't because we were thinking of documentaries. Ken and I were very
> influenced by Brecht at the time and we were interested in a sort of
> alienation effect on film where what was going on on the screen would get
> the *feelings* of the audience, and what was coming on the soundtrack would
> get the *mind* of the audience – it was trying to do that.[107]

65

The strategy becomes clearer if, once again, one compares the
film with the screenplay. To take one example: in the screenplay, the
scene where we first see Reg and Cathy as newlyweds in their new flat is
introduced by a voiceover recording Cathy's pleasure at the affluence of
her new surroundings. The device of using Cathy to establish a scene is
one that Sandford uses several times. However, Loach's preference is *not*
to use establishing shots, or any similar device, but to take the viewer
into the scene first, leaving questions of time, space/place and action to
be resolved later, if at all. In the film, the scene begins with Cathy being
chased by Reg along a veranda outside the flat accompanied by gales of
laughter and shouting. The voiceover is displaced to the end of the
scene, and is heard over a pan down the front of the building, which is
shot romantically, through leaves and branches.

The new opening to the scene in the flat is part of a directorial and editing system of disruption as a means of moving between one scene and the next, of abrupt juxtapositions rather than smooth transitions. The casual, low-key marriage proposal is disrupted by the noise of the wedding, which is then undercut by the pathos of Grandad, now back in his flat and fixed in his chair while his future is being determined by others around him. This scene, which ends with a slow zoom into a close-up of Grandad's tearful face – perhaps the first moment in the film that indicates what is to come – ends abruptly with a sharp cut to Cathy and Reg in their new flat, in the scene under discussion. This does not make the film a formalist exercise, but it does suggest that the filmic structures of the narrative, influenced by modernism, make, as Caughie argues, 'the boundaries between certain forms of naturalism and certain forms of modernism ... thinner and more permeable than the polemics have allowed'.[108]

Afterword: Whose Film is *Cathy Come Home*? Questions of Authorship

One theme in this chapter has been the discrepancies between different versions of the story, in particular the differences between the screenplay and the film. This raises questions about who the author of the different iterations of *Cathy Come Home* is. Sandford was very sensitive to any suggestion that he was not the main author of the drama, even in its final form. In a letter to Madeleine MacMurraugh-Kavanagh, he argued thus:

> In the case of 'Cathy' ... I would submit that the author's voice is strong. The film is based on years of research and on experiences the author had and on a crusading mission the author was mounting. The author chose most of the locations and tape recordings made by the author are used throughout the film. Some (very few) scenes are improvised, often from ideas supplied by the author on the set.

> The director sometimes intrudes too much, I believe. Scenes which
> could have been suggested at script conference are instead improvised on
> location and are of a less high standard, I believe, than the vast majority of
> the scenes that are written directly by the author.[109]

The use of the third person here might have been a way of tempering
personal criticism of Loach, since Sandford spoke warmly of their
collaboration on other occasions. Certainly, Loach worked closely with
Sandford on the script, persuading him to remove the first third, which
focused on Cathy's arrival in London, entirely. This was reflected in an
additional fee in recognition of his contribution (Loach received £300
instead of £200).[110]

Clearly, it is difficult to disentangle who did what on the script,
but the question of who wrote what lines is only one concern among
several. The project was essentially Sandford's: the key ideas, motifs,
much of the language, narrative incident and all of the research were his.
However, the eventual narrative structure – the ordering of incidents,
the system of dislocations and transitions analysed above – was Loach's,
and this is one reason why the published screenplay is very different
from the film itself, and not just in the ways that screenplays are often
different from their realisation on screen. Sandford was sensitive to
what he saw as the encroachments on his rights, and argued that many
of what seemed to be 'filmic' moments were, in fact, his idea.

Perhaps Sandford can be forgiven for thinking that he became
marginalised after *Cathy Come Home*. The BBC continued to pay
Loach a portion of the authorial rights – one third, according a letter in
Sandford's archive – when they were due. Loach and Garnett continued
a fruitful and influential partnership, but with other writers. Sandford
had one more major success, *Edna, the Inebriate Woman*, which was
directed by Ted Kotcheff and produced by Irene Shubik, and which
centred once more on the homeless, this time with an unsympathetic,
elderly alcoholic woman as its protagonist. The play won awards, but
was to be the last time Sandford had a major television commission.

3 Showing and Telling: Visual and Aural Politics and Performance

It is important to the political effect of *Cathy Come Home* that it did not simply talk about society but showed it. In filmed realist drama, the camera, as we have seen, leads the viewer through the studio walls into the streets and houses that are otherwise represented only metonymically, and this is central to its politics. In this way, *Cathy* invites comparison to British realist cinema of the late 1950s and 60s in its concern with showing the immediate situation of the British working class. However, the differences are perhaps more illuminating than the similarities.

The visual style of New Wave cinema was often self-consciously 'poetic'.[111] Walter Lassally, the cinematographer on both *A Taste of Honey* and *The Loneliness of the Long-Distance Runner* (1962), remarked that what made realist films notable is not that they 'treat working-class people, working-class problems, but that they have a very poetic view of them'.[112] 'Poetic realism' captures the double appeal of the visual imagery of realist cinema at the time. On the one hand, it was lauded as 'realist', showing a social reality that had rarely appeared on the post-war cinema screen in meticulous detail: on the other, it was self-consciously 'beautiful', shot in a way that drew attention to its formal composition and aesthetic appeal. The view of the back streets and decaying industrial landscapes in *A Taste of Honey*, for example, frequently treats them in terms of the interplay of architectural forms – arches, the straight lines of trams and railway lines, the sharp right angles and dark surfaces of buildings, implacable against the softness of the humans that stand in front of them. Poetic realism is a response to the aesthetic potential of the photographic image on the big screen; these are, above all, films for the cinema. It is, however, absent from *Cathy Come Home*, which was shot with the documentary photographer's concern with the immediate subject, with close-up and with an awareness of the limited visual appeal of the small screen. This is partly because, as a black-and-white television play from the mid-1960s, the visual is technologically and aesthetically subordinate to the aural, and spectacle is of much less importance than language. There are very few long shots in *Cathy* and only one pan across the city. This occurs early in the film when Reg takes Cathy onto scaffolding attached to a semi-derelict building in a 'totter's yard' (scrapyard) in order to propose to her. While the camera catches the outline of buildings on the horizon, little is made of it, and the attention is quickly directed elsewhere. For most of the film, the camera is at street level and close to what is being filmed, creating an intimacy and immediacy that replaces spectacle and aesthetic distance. Most of all, the environments caught by Tony Imi's observational camera are densely *peopled*, and we are not invited to stand outside them and look in.

Cathy Come Home also denies the poetic in another sense, avoiding visual metaphors or symbols for the most part, and in this it differs from much New Wave cinema. To take an example that illustrates a difference of both method and intention, *Cathy*'s urban landscapes are filled with children, mostly at play. The sequence in which Cathy and Reg come to live with Reg's mum in her overcrowded flat contains extensive shots of children in the courtyard below the tenement, especially where voiceovers replace dialogue, and the drama shifts into observational and documentary mode. Similarly, the Ward family's life in a caravan is documented partly by voiceover, mostly vox pop, over a visual track of children at play among the caravans and in

nearby woods. A parallel might be drawn with *A Taste of Honey*, which also uses children to populate its urban settings, often insistently so. However, the children in Richardson's film are drawn into the narrative of the central character, Jo. As the story often reminds us, at sixteen Jo is little more than a child herself. Her pregnancy and the birth of her mixed-race child propel the narrative of the latter part of the film, which is played out partly in terms of Jo's relationship with the children who fill the streets around her home. There is a good/bad binary opposition between children and adults that works as metaphor and structures the moral world of the film. The symbolic association of childhood with innocence, spontaneity and virtue is emphasised by the soundtrack of a chorus of children singing a familiar playground song, 'The Big Ship Sails on the Alley-alley-oh', which is used on several occasions, notably to conclude the film.

The unnamed children in *Cathy Come Home* have no such immediate or metaphoric relationship to Cathy, and, montaged against voiceover of different kinds, belong much more to the sociological than the dramatic discourses of the film (even Cathy's own children, though central to the dramatic narrative, are 'problems', merely by being alive in an unjust and unequal society and born into a poor family). However, these sequences yield no easy meaning, since the shots of children playing have no direct relationship to the content of the voiceovers and the political and sociological point is not made directly. One possible reading is to see these children as part of a 'normalising' strategy in *Cathy Come Home*. They are filmed at play, humanising their environments as they come to fill them, yet do not acquire metaphorical resonance so much as counter the idea of children as victims: they survive and thrive in situations that challenge some of the stereotypical associations of poverty and the poor.

One of the paradoxes of *Cathy Come Home* is that its use of film meant that it is what it shows of British society that seemed most striking; however, it is often through the voice, or voices, of its largely unnamed collective of characters that the drama makes its most telling points. *Cathy*'s highly populated environments, taken with the use of personal testimony as voiceover, mean that the spoken word, the aural texture of the drama, assumes importance, competing with the visual for explanatory power. It is the people who populate the narrative who give the clearest indication of where the action is taking place. To put it bluntly, we know we are in London because Reg, his family and friends speak in working-class, London accents, and this is confirmed by the accents of those who appear unseen on the soundtrack: and we know we are in Birmingham because the people with whom the Ward family come into contact speak predominantly in Birmingham accents (this includes the housing official who puts them on the council house waiting list). The caravan site, in keeping with its status as a 'non-place', or place where different identities collide, offers a variety of accents. However, those who speak at the meeting of the nearby Ratepayers' Association are southern middle-class. Politically, it seems appropriate that places

73

should be made knowable through the people that inhabit them, since this is a narrative that is wound tightly around the plight of people, individually and collectively.

The various voiceovers provide the best examples of the political and social weight that voices add to the film's narrative. To take an example from the latter part of the film: when Cathy and her children are admitted into hostel accommodation, they are led from the outside into the bowels of the building and then to their room in a sequence that lasts about four minutes. The sequence has five scenes in it, and includes dialogue and two kinds of voiceover (which will be referred to as VP – personal testimony, or vox pop – and VA, the 'voices of authority'):

1. The camera follows Reg away from Cathy and out of the hostel grounds. As Reg leaves through a door from an enclosed courtyard, voiceover one (VA1) begins and continues over the second scene;
2. Cathy and the children at a table in the hostel, shot from a high camera. A second voice (VA2) begins and carries through to the end of the scene.
3. The scene cuts to a blanket room, in which the nurse gives Cathy bedding and the children are stripped prior to disinfection. This scene is covered by dialogue.
4. What follows is one of the more memorable shots in the film, in which the camera leads Cathy and her children up a long staircase and (after a cut) along a corridor peopled with other residents. It is

74

covered by VA3, VA4 and VP1 (on the stairs) and by VA5 and the cacophonous sound of the hostel corridor.

5. The sequence concludes with Cathy and the children led into their room. It is shot from outside the door. Cathy begins a rudimentary unpacking and closes the door on the hostel and on the camera. The sound takes the viewer back into the reality of the room.

The voiceovers are worth considering in detail[113] and quoting in full:

> VA1 (male): Many social workers feel that all homeless families are problem families. They may not be when they arrive in our hostels but they usually are when they leave.
> VA2 (male): It was considered that if a man couldn't provide for his wife and children he wasn't much good. But that is certainly not true today. The great majority of the homeless families we deal with are decent citizens, and all they want is a home of their own.
> VA3 (male): There exists in local authorities a kind of punitive attitude which means that the whole problem of homeless families is the Cinderella of the Cinderellas.
> VP1 (male): So I came out of the welfare place and I said goodbye to the missus, not knowing whether I would see her again. Some men don't seem to be bothered whether they're living with their wife and all that, but I mean I have always been one. We've been happy together and been married eighteen years. I mean you get like that it upsets you, breaks your heart.

VA4 (female): Bus drivers, lorry drivers, coalmen, GPO sorters, general
labourers, scaffolders, all sorts of groups of workers have become
homeless.
VA5 (male): In such times we either build houses in the areas where there
is work. Or we redistribute the work to those areas where there is empty
houses. We're bound to get homeless families. In view of this, it often
seems amazing to those of us who work in this department that there aren't
tens of thousands of homeless families instead of just thousands.

77

The distinction between different kinds of voiceover can be understood
as one between personal testimony and sociological explanation: the
former, a discourse of authentication, with people like the Wards giving
voice to similar experiences and thereby guaranteeing the 'truth' of the
narrative, and the latter a discourse of explanation, coming from outside
the story to account for, and comment on, other discourses, including
that of Cathy herself as revealed in her voiceover. There are a few
exceptions to this general rule. As Reg boards up the windows of the
derelict house, from which the family are about to be thrown out, a
voiceover gives a defence of the eviction from the point of view of the
company managing the property, which is one of very few statements
that seek to justify the status quo.

However, the distinction between the sociological and the
personal does not fully explain what is being attempted by
contextualisation of this kind. For one thing, it is significant that the

majority of VPs in this sequence are male; indeed, the majority of 'voices of authority' throughout the film are male, and there is an unquestioned assumption that male voices will be linked more readily to institutional power and be more persuasive as a result. Conversely, most, though not all, of the personal testimonies are from those who generally hold families together – the women.

The authority of the VP voiceovers comes from the fact that the speakers are more articulate (those sharing their problems do not tend to speak in complete sentences) and talk from a position outside the immediate situation – one that is more likely to be read as objective. They are also more obviously middle class, when performance and delivery are considered. While we can assume that the personal testimony, in this sequence and elsewhere, is spoken by the person who gave it, no such assumption can be made of the voices of authority. Although actors are not credited in the records, it is likely that some at least are used (as Leigh has noted, the distinctive voice of George Sewell, who played a significant role in *Up the Junction*, can be heard throughout the film, and is a contender for VP5). More significantly, it is clear that the voices of authority are not the disembodied narrative voices familiar from dominant forms of television documentary. They are situated within the narrative world, in the sense that they belong to people who implicitly, and sometimes explicitly, identify with the problem of homelessness from a particular institutional perspective and are concerned about it (note the reference to 'our hostels' in VA1 above, and to 'those of us who work in this department' in VA5). They are inside the system for managing homelessness, the welfare state, and are as much a result of Sandford's research process as the personal testimonies. Similarly, the personal testimony in this sequence and elsewhere is often reflective, looking back on both individual experiences which are sometimes related to a general situation ('some men don't seem to bother about whether they're living with their wife') and addressed to the viewer, much as the voices of authority are. Sandford argued that the interviews were often given with an awareness of the audience watching at home.

Who are they talking to? Originally they were talking to me as I recorded them, but they also knew that I would be using them in a documentary which would be addressed to the public. Therefore I think these voices reflect their owner's awareness that they are talking to society as a whole about their predicament.[114]

The essential distinction between these voiceovers, therefore, is between those who administer the system and those who are caught up in it as clients and victims, and even when the text does not make it clear, this is true of most of the voiceovers throughout the film.

The Politics of Institutions

Although *Cathy Come Home* does not interrogate the political structures that create and sustain the housing crisis, it does represent the institutions that manage it. The Wards are taken on a journey through different levels of the housing system, encountering the private rented sector, local authority housing (although she and her family do not ever succeed in obtaining a council flat) and, most tellingly of all, hostels for the homeless. Although this is not represented as a 'system' as such, the voices of authority on the soundtrack frequently draw attention to the failures of the housing process, as the example quoted above reveals. More tellingly, different stages of the journey are represented through interviews with officials of different types, and with different degrees of power, and these become the means by which the institutions that manage housing are humanised. As if to reinforce the relationship between the Wards, it is Cathy who negotiates these interviews (with only one exception, when they first enter the hostel). The way in which *Cathy* represents officialdom has been the subject of much comment, both at the time and since. It was assumed in much of the press comment that the film is uniformly hostile to the officials that Cathy encounters, but this is not what was intended. Loach has argued that the officials 'weren't unsympathetic' or 'the villains of the piece', although 'some

79

were more sympathetic than others. By and large we were very sympathetic to the people who had to administer the unworkable situation that existed.'[115]

The degree of sympathy afforded each official relates in part to the stage in the process of decline at which we encounter them. This relates to a strategy that critics[116] have noted in Loach's later films of seeing the state, in all its various forms, from the protagonist's point of view: if he/she feels threatened or bullied, then this will be reflected in the way that authority figures are represented. While this does not hold true in a specific sense – there is a distance between how Cathy feels about her situation and what we see of how she is treated – there is a general correlation between Cathy's increasingly desperate situation and the attitude of those in authority whom she encounters.

Once Cathy realises she is pregnant, for example, she visits an estate agent (played by Geoffrey Palmer). The scene is almost like an informational short, in which the viewer is educated via carefully structured questions and answers about the mechanics of the house-buying process: as it is explained to Cathy, so it is to us. The scene's focus is mainly on Cathy and it is shot largely from a viewpoint to the right of the agent's right shoulder, with the camera affording a reverse shot of him towards the end, before returning to Cathy. Starting in mid-shot, the scene ends in close-up. The scene is at the service of the points being made, and there is no sense of a shooting strategy that follows Cathy's growing disappointment or seeks to replicate it visually. Later, once the Ward's have gone to live in Birmingham, Cathy visits a housing official, who explains the points system (the way in which housing needs are prioritised) and puts their name down on the housing list for a flat on the Smithson Estate. He is realistic, but not unsympathetic, and promises to see if he can move them up the waiting list in recognition of the seriousness of their situation. The scene is shot largely from Cathy's point of view.

The accusation that *Cathy Come Home* demonises officials is levelled mainly at how they are represented once the Ward family have entered the hostel system. Certainly, one of the ways in which the viewer

knows that this is the end of the journey for the family is the attitude of those who administer the hostels system towards their clients. There are officials of different kinds represented at this point: those who admit people, those who review cases and judge who will stay, go and who will lose their children, and the nurses who are charged with day-to-day support and management. What makes these scenes so chilling is the assumption among those who administer the system at every level that people who enter the hostels for the homeless are failures rather than victims – an assumption that the film manifestly aims to challenge. *Cathy* aligns itself with the views of housing charities and campaigning groups, who argued that official attitudes towards the homeless were shadowed by inherited Victorian notions of the 'deserving' and 'undeserving' poor, with the homeless placed mainly in the latter category. As Des Wilson, the first Director of Shelter, the housing charity

most often linked with the film (see Chapter 4) argued: 'the character of the homeless has been falsified, and the authorities able to infer that the homeless form a small group that would inevitably end up in the cesspool of any society'.[117]

Cathy Come Home represents institutional authority in two main ways. First, the power relationship between clients and administrators (including nurses) is unmasked, with the clients in the role of supplicants asking for favours and expected to be grateful for whatever is handed down to them. This is evident in the ways in which the hostel system works. Reg and Cathy have to wait more than six hours to be processed on entering Cumbermere Lodge, and the sharp, middle-class accent of the unidentified official (Charles Leno), which suggests a military background, makes the social divide brutally clear. 'It must be strictly understood,' he says towards the end of the interview, 'that this is only temporary. After three months, make no mistake, we turn you out.'[118] Later, Reg is summarily ejected from the premises (husbands are only allowed limited visiting rights in the evenings) and is not allowed to show Cathy to her room. Second, officials do not simply explain the rules by which the hostel is run, but also embody its values and ideologies, treating as 'obvious' common sense what the film has called into question. The Warden who admits them brusquely states:

> In lots of places in Britain they don't keep families together. They break
> them up straight away when they become homeless. ... If we rehoused

82

homeless families, then everyone would see an easy way to jump the queue. So we can't do it for obvious reasons.

Although this is the part of the film that often draws the sharpest emotional response, and which had the most immediate effect on contemporary audiences, it maintains the film's overall stance of low-key objectivity. This, in turn, makes it easier to see the events as the product of a system rather than simply the actions of individuals. Although the content of the hostel sequences makes it is impossible to regard it impassively, the camera and narrative do not take the route of aligning the viewer with Cathy's point of view. In a key scene, Cathy is informed by the warden of Cumbermere Lodge that she is to be transferred to Part III accommodation. The interview is shot over the shoulder, largely from the point of view of the interviewing panel of two men and a woman. It begins with a patronising restatement of the situation and the reasons for transfer, which confirms Cathy's powerlessness. 'We could turn you out and take your children into care just like that,' the Warden reminds her. Later in the interview, Cathy learns that they have lost their place on the waiting list for the flat on the Smithson Estate, having moved away from the area; 500 families have moved in already. The irony of the situation, which the audience are aware of but the characters are not, is that the problem that the new housing was designed to solve, the Ward family's homelessness, has meant that they cannot take advantage of it. Her unthinking response is to lose her temper, accusing the panel of laughing at her behind their hands (the scene is still at this point shot from the panel's point of view). There is no evidence for this in the film – we neither see nor hear laughter – but Cathy is responding as much to the general situation as to the specific and imagined slight. The camera does not align us with Cathy through a system of looks and cuts, but it is hard not to be moved by it nonetheless. Once Cathy has left the room, a panel member asks if there is anything further that could be done to help. The response is that the Lodge 'has reached the state that if there were two more families come in tonight we'd have to evict from here to make room for them'. In

83

focusing on the values by which the system is run, *Cathy Come Home* presents officials who appear heartless, but are acting – as they see it – in the interests of a system that is rational and ultimately benevolent; in challenging this, the film's intention is to show a bad system and not 'bad people'. However, officials are not allowed to escape without criticism, for they are required to make the system work, and even if they 'don't make the rules', they enforce them and, it is implied, make harsh and damaging decisions as a result.

'Every person seemed so real': Realist Acting

'Absolutely wonderful – every person seemed so real'. Everything was said to be so convincing about the performance that viewers felt it to be 'actually happening', 'the illusion was complete'. Carol White as the young wife Cathy was praised again and again as really excellent in a part she played with deep understanding and feeling ('At the end of the play her despair reduced me to tears. Definitely a great performance'). Ray Brooks as her husband also acted brilliantly, according to many accounts. The production of the play with its many telling scenes filmed on location was placed in the highest category by a substantial majority of the sample – 'the realism was quite exceptional'.[119]

This quotation is the last paragraph from the BBC's Audience Research Report for *Cathy Come Home*. It demonstrates clearly that the audience valued the acting highly, and responded emotionally to it. They did so, as is so often the case with television drama, by applying criteria of realism, recognising that performance is often where the struggle for authenticity and credibility is won or lost. It is in the performances, as much as the observational, documentary camerawork, that the film's claims to represent the 'real' in social reality can be found.

Undoubtedly, critical and viewer praise for the realism of the acting was shaped by the fact that it looked different to most other acting on the television screen. However, it is very difficult to discuss acting critically, and the analysis of performance, or what actors do in the film-making process, is an under-researched area of television studies (the scholarship of Caughie, Adams, Durham and Cornea not withstanding[120]). What is it that we are looking at when we are looking at an actor? Are we seeing a character, or an actor? And under what conditions might we become aware of one rather than the other? The problem is particularly acute for realism, since the impact of a 'credible' performance relies on the viewer not being too aware of the actor at all. The actor working within this tradition, which constitutes the 'common sense' of television acting, is successful to the degree to which he/she can efface themselves in the role, concealing the work that is being done, reacting 'spontaneously' in the moment and displaying a technique of 'no-technique' (although audiences are clearly aware, as the BBC Audience Survey suggests, of the actor when reflecting on the experience afterwards). Acting is also embedded in the other meaning-making elements of the text – costume, light and other components of *mise en scène* – and actors on screen are subject to the mediation of technology and editing in a way their stage counterparts are not: they are 'done to' as well as 'doing', and much film theory since Kuleshov has privileged editing and montage over acting as the main producer of meaning in screen performance.[121] To turn this round – to analyse the documentary gaze in *Cathy Come Home*, or the impact of Sandford's contextualisation, is also to talk about the actor and acting and much of the preceding discussion has, without acknowledging it, done just this. Finally, it is sometimes impossible to tell on the evidence of the film alone what the contribution of an actor to a particular moment, scene or characterisation actually is, which is why extra-textual information is often important – the comments of director, producer and actor, for example. The following will not attempt to resolve these issues, but will, hopefully, be aware of the difficulties for analysis that they cause.

Both Loach and Garnett have been actors, and respect the way that actors work. Loach has been consistently supportive of actors, and his working methods are, at one level, designed to help actors give the best performances they can. 'I have a great respect for actors,' Loach said in the course of a television interview, 'I enjoy their processes.'[122] Elsewhere, he has observed that his time as an actor in the provincial repertory system helped: 'I saw how actors worked well and how they worked badly and their fears and their anxieties. I learned a lot about their process and what makes it work and how to facilitate it, and about the good and bad things actors can do to each other.'[123] One of many lessons that Loach and Garnett took from Joan Littlewood was her insistence that the realism of a text – play or film – resides primarily in the moment of performance, the here-and-now of the actors in relation to each other, and not just in the *mise en scène*.

Loach's working practices are fairly well known, developed over more than forty years' experience as a director, and aim to support actors' contribution to the process. There are variations, of course, but the following are the main elements: shooting in sequence as far as possible and, therefore, adhering to the chronology of the narrative;

withholding information from actors, so that they only know as much as the character would know at a given point in the story, and can play the scene with a full awareness of the possible outcomes; casting in relation to the general fit between the actor's social class and that of the part he/she will play; casting (some) actors from non-standard backgrounds, with unorthodox training, or no training at all; using improvisation both in rehearsal and in front of the camera (although Loach maintains much less improvised material finds its way onto the screen than is thought); shooting in 'real' locations, with (as far as possible) natural lighting and preserving ambient sound.

Significantly, many aspects of Loach's working process were developed in the mid-1960s, often in response to the need to shoot the film rapidly and under great pressure, and inform the making of *Cathy Come Home*. Loach noted later that the shooting style he developed with cameraman Tony Imi – handheld or single camera on tripod, simple lighting, continuous shooting as far as possible – was designed 'to give the actors freedom' and was 'very much an exploration as we went on, day-by-day'.[124] 'Freedom' in this context valued the actor's contribution to the film-making process but also required a commitment to the realism of the situation: working process and aesthetic ideology were mutually supportive. The intensity that resulted meant that Carol White was rarely able to escape the character and situation she was portraying, and her ability to respond to pressure was valued by the film-makers. 'One of the things that makes Carol good,' Loach observed, 'is that ... whatever we threw at her, she just absorbed and portrayed.'[125] Sandford noted that 'Carol White lived the part of Cathy and was becoming more demoralised and depressed as the play progressed.'[126] Tony Garnett wrote to White's agent, praising her commitment to the role: 'I have been watching rushes every day for the last three weeks and I am knocked out by the quality of the performance. It must have been a very arduous time for her because she is in nearly every scene ... For what little it is worth, I think she has a rare talent.'[127]

87

It is often assumed that the realism of Loach's films results from the fact that he casts non-actors, although this is only partly true.

Loach has on occasion cast people without acting training or previous experience in key roles (although one suspects that this would not, in his view, make them 'non-actors') and often used locally recruited people in small parts or as extras. More often, he has cast actors from unorthodox backgrounds, partly because, in the 1960s especially, both he and Garnett were a little suspicious of professionally trained actors, who might have technique but little sympathy or understanding of the class experience of the people they were portraying. Also, they did not cast 'stars', whose familiarity would intervene between viewer and character, with consequences for realism.

Cathy Come Home was cast largely from actors with whom Loach had already worked, and most had established careers. The large cast was supplemented by actors recruited from the places represented in the film. Some of the memorable but incidental characters on the caravan site, for example, were people who lived on the site being used for the location: and many of the residents of the hostels, in which Cathy and her children find themselves, were people who actually lived there. When Cathy was being cast, Carol White, who was of working-class origins (the daughter of a rag and bone man), was married and bringing up two children in south London. White had worked with Loach on two prior occasions. She played Sylvie, one of the trio of young women at the centre of Up the Junction, and soon afterwards appeared in another Wednesday Play, Jimmy O'Connor's The Coming Out Party (1965). White was an established actress, who had been a child actor, appearing as the five-year-old Sibella in Kind Hearts and Coronets (1949) and in several British films of the 1950s, including Doctor at Sea (1955) and Carry on Teacher (1959). White saw herself primarily as a film actor, and went on to make Poor Cow (1967), Loach's first feature film as director, before pursuing a fitful and unsuccessful career in Hollywood. In retrospect, it is difficult to see another actress in the role of Cathy, so identified with the film did White become. Her casting, however, did have an element of pragmatism to it. Sandford has written that 'Afterwards, with hindsight, I sometimes think, "Oh, yes, of course I always wrote 'Cathy Come Home' for Carol White," but the truth is she was always one of a number of possible stars. When the decision was made, we chose Carol partly because she had two children of her own who were ideal for playing her children in the film.'[128]

Ray Brooks had worked mainly in television prior to being cast as Reg in *Cathy*, but was familiar to the mid-1960s public as one of the main characters in Dick Lester's cult film adaptation of Ann Jellicoe's play, *The Knack* (1965), appearing alongside Rita Tushingham and Michael Crawford. Loach later commented that Brooks had 'exactly the young optimism and enjoyment of life we wanted', with a 'stupid optimism about him that is always more touching than when he sees himself as a victim, even though he is'.[129] Other actors had, similarly, appeared in television or film, and several had worked with Loach before. Wally Patch, for example, who played Reg's grandad, was an experienced character actor, familiar to some of his audience at least from British film comedies, who had also appeared in *The Coming Out Party*.

It is hard to separate different kinds of actor, professional and non-professional, experienced or novice, on the evidence of the film itself, especially as several sequences contain all of these. Yet the inclusion of 'non-actors' is also part of the documentary discourses in the play, and their status as 'actors' is a point at issue. The presence of documentary strategies in the dramatic frame – the observational camerawork and the vox pop voiceover in particular – problematises the reality status of non-professional actors, since the person/actor signifies not only a character in the narrative but also a historical subject, located in the world of the audience as well as that of the narrative. (This is a source of some of the anxiety that is produced by documentary-drama forms.) Additionally, they appear mostly as collective subjects – residents of a housing estate or a hostel – unnamed and 'standing in' metonymically for others in their class and situation. The function of the vox pop, which dominates key sequences as we have seen, is similar.

Taken together, non-professional actors and the vox pop soundtrack can be read as a benchmark of reality in the film, against which other kinds of acting, including that of the main protagonists, are

89

valued. Indeed, there are several occasions when the main characters are filmed in a way that equates them with the documentary/historical subjects directly. For example, there is a short sequence of the Ward family walking the streets shortly after they have been evicted, which is shot in close-up with a handheld camera, covered with a voice of authority reciting statistics on homelessness. Realist acting, therefore, is judged within a documentary frame, and is a clear example of one way in which the dramatic and documentary modes of film-making support each other in *Cathy Come Home*. It is also one reason why such acting within Loach and Garnett films is often equated with notions of truth and the political viewpoint of the play, and is often experienced as 'non-acting'.

This kind of acting-as-documentary is also a complement to, and not in contradiction with, the more formalist/modernist elements in the directing and editing already discussed. Loach has commented perceptively on this in several contexts. In reply to a television interviewer, who had asked him about the tension between naturalism and non-naturalism in his work at this time, Loach argued:

There is a confusion here. It was never an interest in getting actors to behave unnaturalistically stylistically for me. It was, perhaps you might take a sequence of stills, but you could still try to make the content of the stills as realistic as possible, or the performances as authentic as possible. … that was the intention. It wasn't to produce some heightened, stylistic kind of performance.[130]

The specific reference is to *Diary of a Young Man* (BBC 1964), an early collaboration with Troy Kennedy Martin and John McGrath, which experimented with a variety of disruptive and non-naturalist narrative techniques including still photographs. In *Cathy* the disruptions are less radical, perhaps, but the concept of the 'snapshot', of the short scene snatched out of context and presented for our attention, is still important and has an effect on the ways in which acting is seen as realist.

92

To take a particular example: early in the film, we witness Cathy and Reg's courtship. It is revealed, rather than developed, through a series of short scenes juxtaposed to build a picture of a relationship: a conversation in a street about a film Reg has seen; kissing under a tree by a river; chatting on a park bench; arguing after a trip to the cinema. These are not dramatic highlights, and no major crises or high-points are represented. Nor is there any attempt to connect the sequences through voiceover. Sandford's script includes two comments from Cathy that indicate, obliquely, how she feels about Reg, but the film omits these. The impression is of a relationship developing through a series of inconsequential events that build incrementally and are consciously de-dramatised and rendered ordinary. The actors do not have the usual opportunities to reveal character and attitude, and are not allowed by the script or editing strategies opportunities to 'win' sympathy or identification. There are no displays of complex emotion, or a single developed scene in which the character's emotional 'journey' can be played.

The kind of acting that Loach works for requires the suppression of conventional technique, although it is often performed by trained actors; and although it may be perceived as an absence of 'acting', this kind of realist performance can be thought of rather as 'anti-rhetorical' acting. *Cathy*'s ultra-realistic acting style is a paradox, since it aims for a deliberate and systematic de-dramatisation, in which the conventional indicators of actor/director intervention and interpretation, or acting technique, are removed. The strategy is most evident in the way that the text is spoken. It is not simply that the language is colloquial – informal and colloquial language is a marker of the contemporary in realism – but that it is 'unstructured' in the act of delivery: hesitations, slips, repetitions are retained, there are few long speeches, or anything that might signify 'a speech' of any kind, and exchanges of dialogue often lack a sense of dramatic shape or underlying purpose. An actor's instinct to find the moments of decision or change, the turning points of a scene, are much less important – at least, they are much less evident on the screen. What replaces it, in

93

Loach's terms, is a moment-by-moment authenticity, in which the 'truth' of the *situation*, and of the characters' response to it, is more important than the development of character in itself, and is revealed in ways that prefer the anti-dramatic. This style is developed partly out of improvisation, which Loach used not simply to generate new text (although the discrepancy between the film and the screenplay suggests that this was one function, with Sandford's active involvement) but also to capture the social meaning, rather than the rhetorical pattern, of the scene.

Anti-rhetorical acting is a result of the sometimes arduous working processes described earlier, which brought the experience of the actors, especially Carol White, closer to that of the characters they portray. This may have produced a paradoxical effect, in which the emotional intensity and precision required for certain scenes was undermined by the de-dramatised approach that dominates (and, perhaps, by the physical exhaustion of the actors). Leigh has argued that *Cathy* is undermined by White's 'limitations as an actor'. With the key scene where Cathy confronts the panel in the hostel and loses self-control in mind, he maintains that 'The scenes in which Cathy is meant to be emotionally authentic in a grandly demonstrative manner fall flat' and 'without a feeling for her acting, and a belief in the character, it is difficult to empathise with her predicament'.[131] Although the judgment may be harsh, Carol White's playing of the more emotional situations later in the film (giving up her eldest son to her mother-in-law is another telling example) lacks the complexity of the earlier scenes – perhaps a product of exhaustion and the requirement to work across different modes of acting. This does not seem to have lessened the impact of the film on its first audiences, however, or compromised their judgments of the realism of White's acting.

Although anti-rhetorical acting is dominant – it is certainly what audiences tend to remember – there are examples of other, more conventional approaches as well. The scene between Cathy/Carol and an estate agent (Geoffrey Palmer), discussed in Chapter 2, in which Cathy asks about the possibility of buying a house, is shot and acted in a manner that evokes a more familiar, scripted scene, in which the main purpose – to reveal the inequities of the house-purchasing system – is laid out with schematic directness. The performance style of the figures of authority generally, especially those in the hostels, is more studied and reads as being more rehearsed. John Caughie has commented on the political dimension to this, noting 'the way, for instance, in which classical acting skills seemed to be reserved for officialdom or authority in a neat reversal where the traditional skills of impersonation came to mean insincerity, and not quite knowing your lines meant you were speaking the truth'.[132]

　　Loach's observational shooting strategy includes close-up, with the camera sometimes much closer into the face than would have been the norm for the time, bringing the viewer close the characters, especially Cathy, and presenting them for our consideration. Close-up was an accepted part of the language of studio drama, as essential to live performance as it was/is to filmed performance, and a response to both the nature of the small-screen image and the intimacy of the domestic setting in which it was received. 'The smaller screen will no doubt

95

continue to affect the tempo of camera movement,' John Maddison argued in his exploration of the television film in *Contrast*, 'and call for the greater use of close-up.'[133] Don Taylor, a producer who championed the values of 'continuous performance' that studio drama made possible, argued that 'obsessive close-up' enabled 'observation from within' and defined 'the true nature of television acting'.[134] The formulation is enigmatic but relates to the ways in which close-up invites empathy and grants access to a character's subjectivity.[135] Quoting Balazs, Dyer notes how the human face seems almost 'outside' culture and beyond the control of the actor (although, as he points out, facial expression is always subject to cultural convention[136]). A recurrent metaphor is of the close-up as a window, transparently rendering the interior life of the actor/character.

However, Cathy's face in close-up is often impassive, shadowed by a blankness that conveys puzzlement and exhaustion. This is not her subjective state so much as her social situation, and another metaphor is needed. Tony Garnett has argued that 'the most interesting

landscape in any film is the human face'[137] and the distinction between the two metaphors is productive, even if neither is finally conclusive. The face-as-window grants access to an interior life, pulling the viewer into the subjective psychological and emotional experience and identity of the character: the face-as-landscape, however, draws attention to the physical properties of the face itself, and the social identity of the character. Of course, close-ups are placed within particular systems of film-making – a close-up within the editing strategies of classical narrative registers differently to one framed by the impersonal and observational 'documentary gaze' that constitutes the main filming strategy in *Cathy Come Home*. In this filming system, the close-ups of Cathy give us a material record of her experience, bearing the traces of social environment as well as personal history, and are historical documents framed by other historical documents (the desolate cityscapes through which she moves, for example).

White's presence, in close-up or otherwise, in the film was important to the way in which it was received, and was controversial at the time, and since. White was undoubtedly attractive in a way that evoked a particular 60s 'look', and bore a resemblance to another blond icon of the decade, Julie Christie, who had recently appeared in *Billy Liar* (1963) and *Darling* (1965). White played up to the image, and was seen as part of the 'swinging London' scene. 'My name was synonymous with the age,' she told an interviewer in 1987. 'The sixties. Swinging London. Long Hair. Mini-skirts. The Beatles. That spectacular tidal wave that carried a new era and a whole way of life across the Atlantic.' A theme of the interview was how she 'lost out' to Christie. 'After my comeback in *Poor Cow* (1967) I was hailed as the new Julie Christie. But if one looks back to 1962, Julie was called the new Carol White.'[138] There is an element of wish-fulfilment here, but it suggests that the parallel between White and Christie was more a rivalry, for White at least, and was part of a general cultural discourse around glamour and London's place at the centre of 1960s popular culture.

White's sexual allure has been the subject of much comment, not least by the producer Irene Shubik, whose insider view of The

Wednesday Play and Play for Today, *Play for Today: The Evolution of Television Drama*, has coloured academic and journalistic accounts since (see Chapter 4). Shubik notes the controversy, using a contemporary review to make her point:

> there were criticisms that the heroine of the play was much more glamorous than her real-life counterpart would ever have been. 'But,' said one reviewer, 'if Cathy had been more realistically portrayed as a foul-mouthed working-class scrubber and her pretty, appealing children been replaced by appropriately snotty-nosed delinquents, then the sympathies of the good, honest, hard-working and decent British people would have remained dormant … like Dickens before him … the play's author has recognized our incapacity to sympathize with people who happen to be ugly or coarse or nasty.'[139]

This is a particularly harsh version of a more widespread unease about the casting of Cathy that says as much about the classist attitudes of its author (a reviewer from the Cambridge University journal *Granta* whom Shubik does not name) as it does about Carol White. Derek Paget has also raised concerns, noting that 'the point at issue is why a group of film-makers should feel it necessary to portray an attractive Cathy in the first place', and arguing that 'the male section of audience must be attracted to Cathy through desire (a common fate for the female at the centre of play and film narratives, and reflective of dominant patriarchal and heterosexual cultural assumptions)'.[140] Sandford was sensitive to the issue, and in his Introduction to the published script observed wryly that '[p]eople often tell me that Cathy was too attractive – a girl as attractive as that could never have become homeless. This is nonsense. I would say that, on average, the girls I've met in Part III Accommodation were more attractive than those outside, although I couldn't say why.'[141] This rather troublingly sexist response misses the point of the criticism – that Carol White's 60s-style attractiveness blurred the political impact of the film by courting an identification based on desire rather than awareness of the social issues. Sandford later admitted that Cathy was a

99

'pre-feminist construct'.[142] However, like most things about *Cathy Come Home*, the issue is more complex than it seems.

White most obviously inhabits a 1960s persona in the early stages of the film. In the short sequence in the first flat that she and Reg share, White/Cathy is costumed in an obviously youthful, affluent style – turtle-necked jumper, slacks; her hair is worn loose, and she is smoking. The opening of this sequence (see above), with its wild chase around the flat, exemplifies a carefree energy that suggests classless youth. The scene works through a kind of idealisation, which was important to Sandford, who wanted to present the young couple in terms that were 'almost like a television commercial [and would] correspond to a perfect dream romance and a marriage as envisioned by many people'.[143] This returns us to the question of Cathy's individuality/generality, to the sense of her as a composite 'type', recognisable as such to the viewer.

Costume is clearly important to the way in which Cathy and Reg are positioned as 1960s types. In later stages of the film – from the point at which the Ward family move to Birmingham – costume becomes equally important, signifying the Ward family's descent through the housing system. At this point, White/Cathy appears in a loose coat and with her hair uncombed. Reg undergoes a similar sartorial transformation, though it is less marked. Cathy will retain this coat in nearly every external shot (and some internal ones) for the rest of the film. It is hard to read this is as swinging London iconography, and

Cathy takes her place alongside other working-class women in front of the camera. While it may be argued that White's natural attractiveness never ceases to be an issue, her performance, and the ways in which she is costumed, work against this, presenting a clear contrast to the opening. That Carol White's face so readily keyed into a wider imagery of the decade, however, is one indication of how powerfully the film connected with its immediate context of reception – to which we will now turn.

4 Contexts of Reception

Cathy Come Home provoked an immediate response, receiving widespread coverage in the press, with follow-up programmes on the BBC. It also received an overwhelming popular endorsement (as measured by the BBC's own audience survey), leading to an unprecedentedly rapid repeat screening. The immediacy of this response suggests that, however experimental and controversial it might have been, it was not entirely unfamiliar. Indeed, *Cathy* did not arrive unannounced: there was an interpretative framework already in place to greet it.

Newman, as we noted in Chapter 1, did not attempt to hide the play in the schedules, mentioning *Cathy* by name when the 1966–7 Wednesday Play season was announced, and connecting it to the realism of *Up the Junction* and of the series generally. Noting in the *Daily Sketch* in August 1966 that The Wednesday Play had been a success with audiences, Newman said, 'We haven't given audiences escapist trifles, and obviously the audience has responded to this.'[144] Robert MacDonald, writing on the same day in *The Scotsman*, identified *Cathy Come Home* as 'in the "Up the Junction" tradition of "agitational contemporaneity"', saying it was 'an indictment of the way Britain handled the problem of the homeless'.[145] This version of The Wednesday Play was a familiar one, and the anthology series, which included, we should remember, a variety of plays with diverse concerns, had by 1966 become identified with its more controversial and social-realist offerings (see Chapter 1).

The reference to *Up the Junction* in MacDonald's article and elsewhere was not coincidental, since that earlier drama created a precise context for *Cathy Come Home*. *Up the Junction* was the first collaboration between Loach and Garnett (although Garnett was script editor rather than producer), with a script by Nell Dunn. It was broadcast on 3 November 1965, almost exactly a year before *Cathy*, and foreshadowed many of the formal innovations that characterise the later drama, especially a use of documentary techniques within a dramatic frame and location filming using sound 16mm.

Up the Junction provoked more overt hostility than *Cathy Come Home*, but this was largely because of its content. The drama is highly explicit about sex and sexuality, and contains, in graphic detail, an illegal abortion, which occasioned a great deal of press coverage (both hostile and supportive). Like *Cathy*, *Up the Junction* tapped into public anxiety about a current social issue and revealed the extent to which the BBC was becoming a battleground for competing social and moral ideologies. Attempts to reform the laws governing abortion were being discussed in Parliament around the time of transmission, and the play was seen as an attempt to influence and publicise the debate (abortion under certain circumstances was legalised two years later). The hostility that the play generated was reflected in the headlines: 'TV Play Brings Biggest Protest Yet' (*Daily Mail*)'; ' "Up the Junction" Storms Rage On' (*Chronicle and Echo*).[146] The tenor of press coverage was by no means uniformly hostile, however, and the overall effect was to keep the play and the issues it raised in the public gaze.

There were two other valuable lessons to be learned from the transmission of *Up the Junction*. Garnett persuaded the BBC to run an edition of BBC2's *Late Night Line Up* (1964–72), an arts-oriented discussion programme, and BBC Home Service's *The Critics*, both broadcast immediately after the transmission of the play (3 November 1965). A planned, and then abandoned, repeat screening in June 1966 was replaced by an edition of the BBC's current affairs programme *24 Hours* (1965–72), which debated abortion law reform. In persuading the Corporation to create a space elsewhere in the schedules, Garnett succeeded in grafting *Up the Junction* and reform of the abortion laws onto the agenda of other kinds of non-dramatic programming, especially news and current affairs. *Cathy Come Home*, similarly, became a television event, a statement in a dialogue carried on across a range of television discourses, with a life beyond the moment of the initial screening. An edition of *Late Night Line Up* devoted to the programme followed the first transmission of the play, and a second trailed the first repeat screening. An edition of *24 Hours*, which interviewed people in the Ward family's situation, followed transmission of the repeat, going head-to-head with ITV's *The Frost Programme* (ITV, 1966–8, 1972–3, 1977, 1993), also concerned with the play.

A second lesson arose from the place of The Wednesday Play in the schedules. Screened directly after the 9pm news, this proximity to the 'real' increased the likelihood that *Up the Junction* would be read predominantly through its social agenda, within an interpretative framework shaped by news and current affairs, and this was well understood by those who made it: as Ken Loach observed 'we had wanted to make programmes and make plays or films that got the same response as when you saw the news because we came after the news'.[147] As MacMurraugh-Kavanagh observed, this was a lesson 'that Garnett in particular would remember during the planning of *Cathy Come Home*'.[148]

105

Like all Wednesday Plays, *Cathy Come Home* was further mediated by announcements in the press, especially the *Radio Times*, immediately prior to transmission. This process was controlled by Garnett, who was uncompromising while holding onto the version of the play as a 'love story' that had been promoted in the BBC. Garnett argued in the press release that *Cathy* is 'about ordinary people [who] want to lead ordinary lives ... [and] the events of the play have actually happened in the course of the last twelve months. See if that makes you proud!'[149] In the *Radio Times*, however, the account was altogether softer. Cathy, we are told, 'is blond and sexy' and 'dreams of settling down, building a home and having some babies' but 'things don't turn out for her quite like that'. The play is 'a simple love story' about events which 'the author Jeremy Sandford has seen with his own eyes'.[150] Sandford's position as witness to the events and situations he depicts in *Cathy Come Home*, and not simply a researcher into them, is an important guarantee of the drama's authenticity and is used frequently by the BBC in its defence.

The Press Reviews

The initial reviews of *Cathy Come Home* were generally positive, and by this point, all Wednesday Plays could rely on national press coverage. References were made to *Up the Junction*, as one might expect, partly to give the reader an idea of the stable it had come from, but also as a way of introducing anxieties – or rather uncertainties – about *Cathy*'s relationship to documentary form. 'So, is it a "play" or a "documentary"?' asked Gerard Fay in the *Guardian*: 'I think it a bit of both.'[151] This uncertainty was echoed in different words across many reviews. Later, charges were raised against Loach and Garnett that their use of documentary forms in the context of a drama deceived audiences about what they were watching, but there is little sense of this among reviewers. The hybrid documentary drama form was not to every reviewer's taste, but confusion about the reality status of the play was not at issue. Sylvia Clayton in the *Daily Telegraph* argued that she 'would have preferred to see a problem of this magnitude treated as a full-scale documentary investigation rather than a tragic individual love story'.[152] Interestingly, the most stringent attack on *Cathy*'s form came from Philip Purser in the *Sunday Telegraph*, who argued not that the documentary elements deceived the audience about what they were watching but that they contaminated *Cathy*'s value as drama: 'I'm sure the play did a great service to social education,' he argued, 'but I am certain it did a terrible disservice to television drama.'[153]

Similarly, the Audience Research Report suggests that viewers, with few exceptions, were neither confused by nor hostile to *Cathy Come Home*'s form. It recorded an unprecedented reaction index of seventy-eight out of a possible hundred (the average for Wednesday Plays in the season up to this point was fifty-four), with overwhelmingly positive comments from individual viewers. The writer of the Report summarised their dominant response thus:

Cathy Come Home made a deep impression on the vast majority as a very striking and disturbing documentary-style play, which highlighted the problem of the homeless in Britain today in such a way as to arouse intense feelings of pity and indignation.[154]

This suggests that 'documentary-style' plays were, if not entirely familiar, then at least unproblematic for the audience.

Overwhelmingly, reviews responded to *Cathy Come Home*'s depiction of the plight of the homeless on its own terms, with several admitting that they were moved or challenged by what it revealed. As is often the case with realist texts, the success of the film's emotional and authenticating strategies was read as a guarantee of its 'truth' and *Cathy*'s depiction of homelessness is never seriously challenged – not in the national reviews at least. A minority of reviewers found 'Cathy and Reg so deserving as to be implausible',[155] and one thought them 'too glamorous to be representative',[156] but most found them 'appealing' and 'credible'.[157] Sometimes critics were moved against their own political affiliations. Peter Black, in a largely positive review in the *Daily Mail*, wrote that it was 'a poster play, its values starkly black and white, borrowing a good deal from the Communist Party line on housing', but concluded that the BBC was right to broadcast it – 'the old Corp did us a service. It should rightly sting us into uproar.'[158]

Criticism of *Cathy Come Home*'s depiction of homelessness was voiced, however, in an unlikely quarter. Laurence Evans, head of the Local Government Information Office, wrote a stinging rebuttal of the play in *The Municipal and Public Services Journal*, which was picked up by the national press as news. Evan's argued the play had simply misplaced its sympathies. 'The play failed', he wrote, 'because of its highly emotional attempt to encourage sympathy for a feckless and

107

irresponsible young couple who entered marriage, took on an expensive flat and started having babies without one whit of thought for the future.'[159] It was also guilty of misrepresenting the role of local authority officials, with the final scene 'savouring more of Hitler's Germany than present-day England'.[160] Evans went on to complain that no mention was made of the other kinds of help that councils can give people threatened with homelessness, or the possible interventions of the Medical Officer of Health, or the actions of local or national politicians, or voluntary organisations – charges which Sandford denounced as irrelevant to the situation he was describing in the play. When the repeat screening was announced, Evans issued a call to 2 million local government workers to watch the play and ring the BBC with a list of 'blunders'.[161]

Evans did not succeed in undermining the credibility of the play, and few other officials came out in support of his point of view. *The Birmingham Post* adopted the novel strategy of interviewing Alderman Frank Griffin, Leader of Birmingham City Council, while he watched the play and recording his response. The rather unedifying results ('They are just puppets strutting across the screen poisoning the minds of the people watching'[162]) were framed by a furious defence of the play by Sandford and a very positive review by the *Post*'s television critic.[163] The somewhat hysterical reaction of Evans and Alderman Griffin may have been because *Cathy Come Home* was, at the time, the most high-profile attempt to scrutinise the workings of the Welfare State for a mass audience. The state, in its local forms, was not used to this degree of attention or criticism, implied or direct.

At the national level, *Cathy Come Home* had a warmer welcome. Several MPs, including the Leader of the Opposition, Edward Heath, asked the BBC for private screenings, and the Labour MP, Frank Allaun, referred directly to *Cathy* during a speech on the Housing Subsidies Bill in the House of Commons on 15 December. The film was shown to 'senior Ministers and Members of Parliament' in the Commons in late November, all of whom 'had been very impressed, and the only criticisms offered were concerned with matters of detail'.[164] Garnett,

Loach and Sandford were invited to the Ministry of Housing to discuss the housing crisis, during which, according to Garnett, the Minister said:

> [t]hey had all been given hell by their wives who had seen the programme and wanted to know what was being done about the homeless ... although the programme hurt, he was delighted that there were still some people left with social consciences.[165]

The only issue that threatened ministerial equanimity was that of the captions over the closing credits, 'particularly the one about West Germany'.[166] The caption singled out runs: 'West Germany has built twice as many houses as Britain since the War.' This was to prove troublesome on different fronts. According to Garnett, the issue was not one of factual accuracy ('We were not challenged at any point on our intentions in making the film or on our facts') but of judgment: the caption was deemed 'unfortunate'. The comparison with West Germany, the defeated enemy in World War II, memories of which were still raw, was undoubtedly provocative. Garnett took full responsibility for its inclusion, noting that he had been strongly advised to omit the caption (indeed, all the captions): 'I said that I may have been right or wrong but it was my decision to ignore the advice and leave the captions in.'[167] This was not to be the end of the matter. Garnett and Loach came under considerable pressure within the BBC to remove all the final captions. In a memo dated 16 December, the Head of Plays, Gerald Savoury, wrote that 'there is a piece at the very end comparing England unfavourably with other countries that I want removed'.[168] Sandford commented later on the strength of feeling, both within and beyond the BBC: 'Later I learned that quite strong pressure had been put on the BBC to not stand firm by the film but instead to admit that it was a fabrication and this sort of thing was not going on in Britain.'[169]

    There has been some debate since as to how the film-makers responded to this pressure. A review in *The Times* after the first repeat screening suggested that 'the line between play and documentary was now more clearly defined by the deletion of most of the spoken

109

background comment'.[170] This assertion, or a version of it, has since passed into several academic and other accounts, although Derek Paget has argued convincingly that no alterations were made for the repeat screening, nor for any subsequent screenings.[171] Garnett was particularly adamant that no changes had been made, and Sandford pursued in print several writers who published the allegations,[172] notably Irene Shubik, whose insider account of television drama in the period is one of the principal sources for the information.[173] (The BBC Worldwide DVD from 2003 contains all the captions and original soundtrack.)

Cathy Come Home was repeated on 11 January 1967, eight weeks after initial transmission, which was unprecedented. It was much anticipated, although the news stories in the prelude to the January screening were largely dominated by Laurence Evans' call, mentioned above, for local authority workers to deluge the BBC with complaints about supposed errors. 'Two Million Try to Trap "Cathy"' was the headline in the Daily Mail, while the Daily Sketch led with 'Town Hall Check on Play That Shocked'.[174] The BBC was called upon to defend the veracity of the play to journalists, and Sandford tirelessly championed it in print and at public meetings in the period between the two screenings. The Daily Mirror article, for example, concluded with a comment from a BBC 'spokesman' that replayed Sandford-as-witness as an automatic defence of Cathy's truth: 'Everything seen in the play has happened, and was seen by the author at first hand.'[175] As MacMurraugh-Kavanagh has argued,[176] internally the BBC was uneasy about the argument of the film, and some of the research it contained, but chose to defend it publically. Undoubtedly, the generally positive press response to the first transmission made this easier, as did the response of Government ministers. Also, Cathy Come Home was never quite as controversial, in the sense of being scandalous (while being about a scandal), as Up the Junction.

In fact, whatever adverse criticism of Cathy might have emerged was outflanked in the pre-Christmas period by other news stories involving BBC drama and two regular headline-grabbers, Dennis Potter and Jonathan Miller. Potter had been commissioned to write an adult version of Cinderella (entitled Almost Cinderella) to be screened over Christmas, but it was withdrawn from the schedules before being made due to concerns about the quality of the script and its suitability for Christmas viewing. Potter had already had a play withdrawn, *Vote, Vote, Vote for Nigel Barton* (BBC 1964), about a Labour candidate in a General Election, which, though it was at least made, was postponed because of the proximity of the allocated screening slot to the date of the British General Election of 1964. In both cases, he was incandescent with rage, threatening, after the BBC's refusal to make *Almost Cinderella*, to quit the Corporation altogether. The *Evening News* reported him as saying 'If I can arrange my career so that I never have to write plays for BBC TV again then I intend to do so.'[177] At the same time, another furore emerged, this time over Jonathan Miller's film of *Alice in Wonderland*, which had a starry cast that included John Gielgud. Scheduled for peak family viewing over the Christmas period, the BBC took a late decision to move it to a later time on 28 December, arguing that its original slot was inappropriate. The initial story concerned the BBC's embarrassment at having to admit that this children's classic was not suitable for children, with a subtext that this was one more example of 'progressive' directors polluting television. After transmission, the press picked up on figures released by TAM, the audience research organisation, which suggested that viewers had switched off in significant numbers: 'TV "Alice" Snubbed by Millions', as Philip Phillips put it in the *Sun*.[178] This second piece of embarrassing news was published by most papers on 10 January, one day before the repeat screening of *Cathy Come Home*, drawing attention and giving potential critics another target.

111

　　　　Press reviews of the repeat were generally positive, especially among TV critics. The headlines give a sense of this: the *Daily Express* review was headed 'Loaded, But it Hurt Like Mad',[179] while *The Times* review appeared under ' "Cathy" Repeat Justifies its Dramatic Validity'.[180] Most reviewers accepted the power of the play to move audiences and depict 'the squalor and despair of the homeless',[181] and acknowledged the public concern that had been voiced in the eight weeks since the first screening. This concern was sometimes used as an answer to the reviewer's own unease about *Cathy*'s form and politics. Stanley Reynolds in the *Guardian*, for example, argued that 'the Sandford play has aroused a general social conscience and therefore the mixed drama and documentary technique seems to have justified itself [and] was if anything understated'.[182]

The importance of the heady publicity generated by *Cathy Come Home* to the generally positive view of the film was made clear in the BBC Audience Research Report for the January repeat. The audience for the repeat was around 12 million (24 per cent of the population), about the same as for the first transmission: the reaction index, however, was even higher, scoring eighty-five out of a possible hundred (as against seventy-eight). It was clear that *Cathy* was even more popular with those seeing it a second time, where the reaction index was eighty-nine, than it was among viewers coming to it for the first time, where it was eighty-three (this is still higher than the original index, itself very high indeed). The percentage of viewers registering negative opinions halved, from 6 to 3 per cent, or, as the Report put it, 'for every viewer who strenuously objected to the Cathy Come Home repeat there were sixty whose reactions were enthusiastic'.[183] The increased reaction index was highly unusual, leading the writer of the Report to conclude that it could only have been a response to the public debate about the play after its initial screening:

112

> It can therefore only be concluded that the reactions of the repeat audience were influenced by the furore created by Cathy in November, though how far it was the public comment and how far word of mouth it is impossible to say.[184]

Cathy Come Home and the Documentary/Drama Controversy: Another Take

The press response to *Cathy Come Home* noted that the play challenged accepted dramatic categories, creating a certain puzzlement which largely evaporated in the face of its emotional power. A similar response can be found in the BBC Audience Research Reports, with the viewers of the repeat screening seemingly less troubled than those of the original one. There is a sense in which *Cathy* acted on its audience in the way that experimental texts sometimes do; that is, the film itself provided viewers with the knowledge and conventions required to understand it. However, this did not mean that *Cathy*'s realist excursions into documentary form ceased to cause difficulties, notably from within the BBC.

On 8 January, the Sunday before the repeat screening, an article appeared in the *Sunday Telegraph* with the title 'Stop Mixing TV Fact and Fiction'.[185] Its author was Grace Wyndham Goldie, former Head of Talks and Current Affairs for BBC Television, a much-respected BBC insider, who it was assumed spoke for many of her former colleagues. It is worth considering this article in detail, since the point of view it promoted was one that has had some currency, at the time and since. Dismissing the play with the epithet 'tear-jerker', Wyndham Goldie objected that what might be seen as a 'once-and-for-all experiment in dramatic television' may be 'an early example of a new and dangerous trend in television drama'. The issue was that in being touted as a 'semi-documentary', *Cathy* 'deliberately blurs the line between fact and fiction'. There are two problems with this, in Wyndham Goldie's analysis. The first is that *Cathy*, and documentary-drama generally, broke faith with the audience who 'have the right to know whether what they are being offered is real or invented'. The second is that, as a 'powerful piece of advocacy', it broke faith with the BBC's Charter (and there can be few transgressions more serious than this), which forbids the Corporation, as well as its commercial rival, to 'use their privileged position to advocate, in areas of controversy, particular policies and courses of action'.

113

These criticisms are voiced from a position that is aware that the consumption of television is different from that of other cultural forms – that the drama's position in the flow of an evening's viewing means that it is likely to be read in particular ways.

> We see on the television screen a succession of images. We expect some of
> them, news and outside broadcasts, current affairs reports and factual
> documentaries, to be an accurate reflection of the real world. If, among
> them, we get a 'semi-documentary' which intermingles the real with the
> fictional and which may, in order to establish a greater sense of reality, use
> film clips from news bulletins or from Panorama or Twenty-four Hours, then
> a doubt could well be cast upon the validity of what has in fact been real.

Of course, *Cathy Come Home* does not use film clips of this kind, rather
it borrows aspects of its visual and aural style from them to shoot
fictional events. Also, questioning the truth claims of television news
and current affairs is, politically speaking, exactly what Loach, Garnett
and Sandford wanted, but this does not amount to confusing the
audience. The argument has institutional resonances, since what irked
Wyndham Goldie and others was the fact that directors, producers and
writers working in the Drama Department did not suffer the same
restrictions on their independence that were placed on their
counterparts in news and current affairs. When Wyndham Goldie wrote
that 'if you put advocacy into the semi-dramatic form of a semi-
documentary it may in effect be by-passing the fundamental rules under
which broadcasting organisations are permitted by society to exercise
their privileges', the responsibilities conjured up, silently in the
background, are those of the journalist towards 'facts'. The repeated
invocation of this argument was one reason why Sandford was so
adamant about the robustness of his research.

In choosing to argue against 'advocacy' Wyndham Goldie was
challenging the right of television drama to engage directly with social
and political issues. It is likely that Wyndham Goldie, and many of her
readers, would have had the example of Peter Watkins' polemical and
controversial re-creation of the aftermath of a nuclear war, *The War
Game*, made and scheduled for screening in 1965, in mind: Watkins'
film combined documentary and dramatic re-enactment in innovative
ways to political effect and was banned, not to be screened on television
until 1985. But as Loach noted, the concerns about the hybridity of

documentary drama were not essentially about its form: 'it is very revealing that their [the BBC's] dispute with us was not with the form, but with what we were saying inside it'.[186]

Cathy Come Home and Shelter

The January transmission of *Cathy Come Home* coincided with another development, which it did a great deal to promote. Several charities for the homeless used the public indignation caused by *Cathy* to enlist public support; however, it is Shelter with whom the play was, and is, most clearly associated. Sometimes it seems as though *Cathy Come Home* and Shelter came from the same womb, their histories are so intertwined. Shelter was, in fact, established one week before the repeat screening as a national body, which had been some time in the making. Conceived as a campaign as well as a conventional charity, Shelter was the brainchild of Bruce Kenrick, a radical Methodist clergyman, who had been the driving force behind the Notting Hill Housing Trust, which had sought to provide a solution to the housing crisis by providing low-cost accommodation for London's poor. Kenrick persuaded a number of other housing charities to suspend fundraising and join a new campaign with a national reach, and Shelter was launched in a blaze of publicity in St Martins-in-the-Fields in London. Des Wilson became Shelter's director, and steered the campaign into its pre-eminent position as the UK's leading national charity for the homeless.

115

While Shelter would have been formed even if *Cathy Come Home* had never been made, it used the film's profile to immediate effect. Kenrick persuaded the BBC to allow Shelter to use a still of Carol White/Cathy in its poster campaign launched the day after the January screening. In the newspapers, the image was captioned thus: 'Did you see Cathy last night?'[187] It was followed by a description of the film, noting that there are 'literally thousands of Cathys in Britain at this moment' and that Shelter was formed 'to do something *now* about the desperate situation that lies just under the surface in this country today'.

The initial campaign proved very successful, raising £50,000 in the first month.

From this point onwards, press coverage of homelessness, and/or Shelter, automatically referenced *Cathy Come Home*, normally by evoking Cathy herself as an iconic and representative figure. Des Wilson began his 1970 account of the early years of Shelter with a chapter entitled 'Whatever Happened to Cathy?', in which he speculated what might have happened to Cathy in the interim (she and her family will, he argued, be either still separated or living in appalling sub-standard conditions in an inner-city slum).[188] Cathy's symbolic potency was such that in 1969, with a General Election near, Des Wilson sought to influence debate about housing policy by writing an article in the *Guardian* in the form of a letter to Cathy explaining that she was 'the victim of a piece of political deception'.[189] Shelter still uses Cathy and *Cathy Come Home* as a point of reference in relating its history on its website.[190]

One of the reasons why *Cathy Come Home* was so important to Shelter was that it represented the problem of homelessness as a *process*, a journey, rather than as a simple state. It also placed this process in the context of local and central government policy and as a consequence of poverty, and was therefore very much in line with Shelter's thinking. In a letter in the *Evening News* published five days after *Cathy*'s repeat screening, Bruce Kenrick wrote that the money donated to Shelter would be used to help not only those who were homeless according to accepted government definitions but also 'the "hidden homeless" – those millions now living, as a White Paper puts it: "In slums, in near slums and in grossly over-crowded conditions"'. The solution he advocates is an urgent renewal of older housing, rapidly deteriorating, largely in private hands and rented to the poor, which will 'rescue great numbers of Cathys'.[191]

Behind Shelter's policy in the late 1960s was the controversial question of how homelessness was to be defined. Des Wilson quoted David Ennals, the Minister of State for Health and Social Security, arguing in 1969 that the homeless figures have been subject to 'a great

116

deal of exaggeration', and that the true figure was 3,594 'families living in temporary accommodation'.[192] The point is not so much the figure as the definition employed to arrive at it. Wilson commented thus:

Excluded from the homeless by most definitions are:

1. Families 'on the streets' – sleeping in an abandoned car, or in the open. (This again shows the absurdity of the official definition; having lost the four walls and a roof, the family have to regain them – 'in temporary accommodation' – before they are homeless!)
2. Families living in squalor
3. Families hopelessly overcrowded
4. Families split up (including those with children 'in care')
5. Families taken in under stress by in-laws or friends
6. Families in physical danger because of the unfitness of their property
7. Families lacking many or all of the essential facilities, toilets, hot water, etc.

117

All of the above families are *not* homeless in the eyes of most authorities.[193]

This list echoes the descent of Cathy and her family through the housing system. At different times, the narrative shows them living in an overcrowded home (Reg's mum's flat), in squalor (almost everywhere once they leave their flat), in an unfit property without facilities (the house they are evicted from) and sleeping in the open air. In this way, *Cathy Come Home* dramatises more than the problem of the 'homeless' narrowly defined, and reveals a system in crisis.

By the end of the decade, Government Ministers were arguing that the situation of the homeless had been contained and was being reversed, although this was contested by the housing charities, including Shelter, and by Sandford. In 1968, *Cathy Come Home* was awarded a Prix Italia, a prestigious international prize for innovation in television. A repeat screening was arranged, and Sandford asked if he would prepare a pre-transmission statement pointing out that many of the statistics no longer applied. In a reply to Gerald Savoury, Head of Plays, who has asked him for the statement, Sandford noted that in some cases, including conditions in Part III Accommodation, things 'have generally got better although ... there have been exceptions'. In other respects, the situation had deteriorated: 'The figure, given in "Cathy", of 4,000 children taken into care each year for no other reason than homelessness has now become 5,000. The figure of 12,500 inhabitants of Part III Accommodation ... has now become 15,000.'[194] By this point in the decade, the sense of crisis in the prevailing social, political and economic consensus was becoming palpable, and the homeless disappeared into the crowd of new historical problems that were gathering at the gates.

Conclusion

This book began by placing *Cathy Come Home* in the context of a general optimism about Britain and its place in the world of the mid-1960s, and arguing that it challenged widespread and influential ideas concerning post-war consensus, classlessness and universal affluence. As the decade progressed, there were many such challenges, as the tensions and contradictions forming beneath the skin of British society broke to the surface, and the new decade arrived: active resistance to British support for the increasingly unpopular US presence in Vietnam; the global counter-cultural revolution that was 'May 68', the summation of the 'decade of youth'; the re-election of right-wing governments across the world in response; a resurgence of racism and fascism in the UK, with the National Front taking the anti-immigrant struggle to the streets and the ballot box; the eruption of virtual civil war in the streets of Northern Ireland, as thirty years of 'The Troubles' began; the return in the 1970s of economic crises; and increased industrial militancy, culminating in the miners' strikes of 1973 and 1974, which provided much of the imagery through which the 1970s has since been interpreted. Much of the left, meanwhile, looked beyond established political forces, on the one hand to the Women's Movement, in its many cultural, political and economic forms, or to British Trotskyism, which was particularly influential in the arts and media.[195]

   In this more revolutionary climate, *Cathy Come Home* seemed much less radical than it had only a few years earlier. Looking back at *Cathy* in the early 1970s, Loach and Garnett were tough-minded in their analysis of what they considered to be the film's political limitations. Interviewed by G. Roy Levin in 1971, Loach argued that *Cathy* was compromised by its very success with politicians of different persuasions:

> The great weakness of it [the film] is that everybody can claim it as their own. You know, every politician can say ... 'This sheds light on the housing problem'. You know, if it can do that, in a way it's kind of terribly failed. Not totally, but it's largely failed, because while it gives an impression of the problem, nevertheless it doesn't lead towards an understanding of what causes the problem.[196]

In the same interview, Garnett was pressed to explain how he would change the film were he to remake it for the 1970s. Noting that Sandford might see things differently, he replied:

> [f]rom our point of view, it would be reframed altogether. It's not just a question of adding a few lines. I think one would take that situation and restructure it, tell the story very differently. One would avoid the situation where an audience could get out of the moral difficulty by blaming a few local officials on the periphery of the system. You've got to blame the system at its base. So one would have to bring more of that into it, and one would also have to make it very clear what the solution to the problem would be, in terms of a political analysis. This would then engage one not just in a discussion of how many houses should be built to what standards, but what is the political and economic structure that is behind all this.[197]

A version of this criticism has attached to *Cathy Come Home* ever since. Loach argued in the late 1980s that *Cathy Come Home* was 'a film about a social situation' and 'not a political film because it doesn't deal with structure at all – the structure of what makes people homeless'.[198] This judgment reserves the term 'political' for a certain kind of analysis, one which does not so much state a problem as explain its underlying causes (a spatial model, of 'surface' and 'depth' is implied here). *Cathy*

Come Home has the clear intention to intervene in public policy debate, and the film provides a way of understanding the reality of a particular social situation, but it is still a snapshot, in Loach's view: the question of how things came to be like that still remains.

In 1971, Garnett went on to argue that a 'new' *Cathy* would need to eschew its appeal to emotion and find an alternative way of engaging its audience politically. 'You weep, if the film gets to you and you say, "Oh, how unfortunate, isn't it a pity that this sort of thing goes on. It's such a shame." But that's not enough ... If people are harmed, tell them what to do about it.'[199] A distrust of emotion seems almost perverse in the context of early twenty-first-century television, where there often seems no other way of engaging an audience's attention, and perhaps the demand that each analysis of a specific social problem become a critique of capitalism seems a little brutal. *Cathy Come Home* has endured partly because of the qualities that frustrated Loach and Garnett – its emotionalism, its obsessive picking away at a particular problem, without recourse to a structural analysis of society. *Cathy* knows its limitations and what can be achieved in the restricted timeframe of a seventy-two-minute drama. It is interesting that when more analytical, discursive dramas appeared, it was in long form – Loach and Garnett's four-part analysis of labour history, *Days of Hope*, for example, or Troy Kennedy Martin's four-part *Edge of Darkness*.

Social realism, meanwhile, has migrated to other dramatic forms, a wellspring (perhaps now dried up) for continuous serials such as *Brookside* (C4 1982–2003) and *EastEnders* (BBC 1985–) and 'cops'n'docs' genre fiction. Some of *Cathy*'s distinctive features have entered the everyday lexicon of UK drama production, in particular its 16mm aesthetic of handheld camera and intense close-up, though shorn of its association with documentary. Born of the fluid, not to say chaotic, conditions of drama production in the mid-1960s, *Cathy* has transcended its immediate context, with its formal radicalism still not fully appreciated. The questions it poses about the housing crisis have not been resolved. As Garnett has observed, television critics once asked 'Where will the next *Cathy Come Home* come from' while studiously avoiding looking at what was actually being made.[200] There is, at this point and others since, a tendency towards 'Golden Ageism', which sees the drama of the 1960s and 70s as the pinnacle of achievement, from which everything since is a falling-off. As the subsequent careers of both Loach and Garnett, and of the many talented and radical people who have made television since, testify, this will not suffice. Rather than simply valorise the film, it is perhaps more pertinent to ask now: what can we learn from *Cathy Come Home*? I hope this book has suggested that the answer is more than we think.

Notes

1 The event was one of several organised to mark the fiftieth anniversary of the journal *Screen* and was organised by the Department of Film and Television Studies at Warwick, *Screen* and the Midlands Television Research Group. A summary and report of the day can be found in *Critical Studies in Television* vol. 4 no. 2, Autumn 2009, pp. 108–19.

2 Quoted by Derek Paget, 'Preface', Jeremy Sandford, Cathy Come Home (screenplay) (London: Marion Boyars, 2003), p. i.

3 I am indebted to John Caughie's Introduction to Edge of Darkness (London: BFI, 2007) for this information.

4 Ibid., pp. 2–3.

5 Christine Geraghty, 'Classic Television: A Matter of Time', *Critical Studies in Television* vol. 4 no. 2, Autumn 2009, p. 109.

6 David Hare, 'How the BBC Killed the TV Play', *The Times*, 25 August 2008.

7 Lez Cooke, *British Television Drama: A History* (London: BFI, 2003), p. 66.

8 Quoted by Dave Rolinson, 'Play for Today', <www.britishtelevisiondrama.org.uk/playfor today/> (last accessed 12 March 2010).

9 See Tony Garnett, 'Contexts', in Jonathan Bignell, Stephen Lacey and Madeleine MacMurraugh-Kavanagh (eds), *British Television Drama: Past, Present and Future* (Basingstoke: Palgrave/Macmillan, 2000), p. 19.

10 <entertainment.timesonline.co.uk/tol/ arts_and_entertainment/tv_and_radio/ article4590364.ece> (last accessed 19 January 2009). Although the article by David Hare is still on *The Times* website, the online forum responses have now been withdrawn.

11 John Seed, 'Hegemony Postponed: The Unravelling of Consensus in Britain in the 1960s', in Bart Moore-Gilbert and John Seed (eds), *Cultural Revolution? The Challenge of the Arts in the 1960s* (London: Routledge, 1992), p. 29.

12 See Michael Pinto-Duschinsky, 'Bread and Circuses? The Conservatives in Office, 1951–64', in Vernon Bogdanor and Robert Skidelsky (eds), *The Age of Affluence: 1951–64* (Basingstoke: Macmillan, 1970), pp. 55–6; also Seed, 'Hegemony Postponed', pp. 22–4.

13 See Stuart Laing, *Representations of Working-Class Life 1957–1964* (Basingstoke: Macmillan, 1986); also Stephen Lacey, *British Realist Theatre: The New Wave in its Context 1956–65* (London: Routledge, 1995).

14 Pinto-Duschinsky, 'Bread and Circuses?', p. 57.

15 Seed, 'Hegemony Postponed', p. 23.

16 Pinto-Duschinsky, 'Bread and Circuses?', p. 62.

17 'London: The City that Swings', *Time*, 15 April 1966.

18 Quoted in Des Wilson, *I Know it was the Place's Fault* (London: Oliphant, 1970), p. 36.

19 For a full discussion of these developments see Cooke, *British Television Drama*.

20 In 1954, the BBC broadcast for just six hours a day, but by the mid-1960s the aggregated BBC and ITV output was sixteen hours.

21 See John Cook, 'Between Grierson and Barnum: Sydney Newman and The Development of the Single Television Play

at the BBC 1963–7', *Journal of British Cinema and Television* no. 2, Spring 2005, p. 216.

22 See Irene Shubik, *Play for Today: The Evolution of Television Drama*, 2nd edn (Manchester: Manchester University Press, 2000), p. 43.

23 John Cook, 'Between Grierson and Barnum', p. 4.

24 Garnett, 'Contexts', p. 13.

25 John Maddison, 'What is a Television Film?', *Contrast* vol. 13 no. 1, Autumn 1963, p. 75.

26 Troy Kennedy Martin, 'Nats Go Home: First Statement of a New Drama for Television', *Encore* no. 48, March–April 1964, pp. 21–33.

27 Ibid., p. 25.

28 Tony Garnett, Letter, *Encore* no. 49, May–June 1964, p. 45.

29 For further discussion see Steve Bryant, *The Television Heritage* (London: BFI, 1989), pp. 6–7.

30 Raymond Williams, 'A Defence of Realism', in Williams, *What I Came to Say* (London: Hutchinson Radius, 1990), p. 232.

31 Raymond Williams, 'Recent English Drama', in B. Ford (ed.), *The Pelican Guide to English Literature No. 7: The Modern Age* (London: Pelican, 1978), p. 498.

32 Williams, 'A Defence of Realism'.

33 Raymond Williams, *Politics and Letters* (London: New Left, 1979), p. 221.

34 John Caughie, *Television Drama: Realism, Modernism and British Culture* (Oxford: Oxford University Press, 2000), pp. 70–1.

35 Leonard Quart, 'A Fidelity to the Real: An Interview with Ken Loach and Tony Garnett', *Cineaste* no. 4, Autumn, p. 28.

36 Madeleine MacMurraugh-Kavanagh, 'The BBC and the Birth of "The Wednesday Play", 1962–66: Institutional Containment Versus "Agitational Contemporaneity" ', *Historical Journal of Film, Radio and Television* vol. 17 no. 3, 1997, p. 367.

37 A full list of Wednesday Plays, along with details of their authors, directors and producers, can be found in Shubik, *Play for Today*.

38 Sydney Newman, 'The Wednesday Play', Memo to Keith Adam, 15 June 1966, BBC WAC T5/695/2, 3798/9.

39 See MacMurraugh-Kavanagh, 'The BBC and the Birth of "The Wednesday Play" ', for a discussion of the ambivalence of the BBC towards the series.

40 For further information on this season and the role of the script editors, see Stephen Lacey, *Tony Garnett* (Manchester: Manchester University Press, 2007).

41 For a full discussion of the first series of The Wednesday Play see Cooke, *British Television Drama*.

42 Jeremy Sandford, 'Introduction', in Sandford, Cathy Come Home, p. 7.

43 Ibid., pp. 8–9.

44 Ibid., p. 9.

45 BBC WAC T5/695/1 *Cathy Come Home*; introduction to the storyline for *The Abyss*, 28 January 1965.

46 Sandford, Cathy Come Home, p. 10.

47 Ibid., p. 11,

48 Jeremy Sandford, commentary in the extras on DVD *Cathy Come Home* (BBC Worldwide, 2003).

49 Quoted in Shubik, *Play for Today*, p. 110.

50 Ibid.

51 Ibid., p. 12.

52 Jeremy Sandford, *Cathy Come Home: The Novel* (London: Pan, 1967), p. 85.

53 Sandford, Cathy Come Home (screenplay), p. 13.

54 In conversation with the author, 24 July 2004.

55 Quoted in Graham Fuller and Ken Loach, *Loach on Loach* (London: Faber and Faber, 1998), p. 23.

56 Jeremy Sandford, 'The Trashing of Cathy', <www.JeremySandford.org.uk> (accessed 24 March 2009).

57 In conversation with the author, 7 October 2004.

58 John Mackenzie, 'When Cathy Comes to Town', Project No. 2116/4369, BBC WAC T5/695/2.

59 Sandford, Cathy Come Home (screenplay), p. 13.

60 Derek Paget, '*Cathy Come Home* and "Accuracy" in British Television Drama', *New Theatre Quarterly* no. 57, February 1999, p. 80.

61 Newman, 'The Wednesday Play', BBC WAC T5/695/2, 3798/9.

62 Shaun Usher, untitled, *Daily Sketch*, 17 August 1966.

63 The schedule is contained in BBC WAC File T5/965/2.

64 Jeremy Sandford, commentary on DVD of *Cathy Come Home*.

65 Ken Loach, commentary on DVD of *Cathy Come Home* (BBC Worldwide, 2003).

66 Jeremy Sandford, 'Edna and Cathy: Just Huge Commercials', *Theatre Quarterly* vol. 3 no. 10, 1973, p. 80.

67 Loach, DVD commentary.

68 Madeleine MacMurraugh-Kavanagh, 'Kicking Over the Traces: An Interview with Tony Garnett', *Media Education Journal* no. 24, Summer 1998, p. 27.

69 For a discussion of these connections see Stephen Lacey, 'Becoming Popular: Some Reflections on the Relationship Between Television and Theatre', in Jonathan Bignell and Stephen Lacey (eds), *Popular Television Drama: Critical Perspectives* (Manchester: Manchester University Press, 2005).

70 For details see Lacey *Tony Garnett*, p. 42.

71 Jeremy Sandford, 'Warp-Aftermath of Cathy', at <www.JeremySandford.org.uk> (accessed 24 March 2009).

72 Ibid.

73 Paddy Scannell, 'The Social Eye of Television, 1946–1955', *Media, Culture and Society* vol. 1 no. 1, 1979, p. 101.

74 Ibid.

75 Jamie Sexton, ' "Televerite" hits Britain: Documentary, Drama and the Growth of 16mm Filmmaking in British Television', *Screen* vol. 44 no. 4, Winter 2003, p. 433.

76 Ibid., pp. 437–9.

77 MacMurraugh-Kavanagh, 'Kicking over the Traces', p. 27.

78 John Corner, '*Cathy Come Home* (1966)', in Corner, *The Art of Record: A Critical Introduction to Documentary* (Manchester University Press, 1996).

79 Kennedy Martin, 'Nats Go Home', pp. 21–33.

80 '*The Abyss* – outline', BBC WAC T5/695/1.

81 Deborah Knight, 'Naturalism, Narration and Critical Perspective: Ken Loach and the Experimental Method', in George McKnight (ed.), *Agent of Challenge and Defiance: The Films of Ken Loach* (Trowbridge: Flick, 1997).

82 Ibid., p. 77.

83 Ibid., p. 78.

84 Ibid., p. 21.

85 Sandford, Cathy Come Home, p. 23.

86 Corner, *The Art of Record*, p. 94.

87 Ibid.

88 Ibid.

89 Michael Walker, 'Melodrama and the American Cinema', *Movie* no. 29/30, Summer 1982, pp. 13–16.

90 Ibid., p. 14.

91 Ibid., p. 2.

92 Ibid., p. 13.

93 Although Walker is discussing American melodrama in this article, he argues explicitly that both *Cathy Come Home* and a later Loach/Garnett collaboration, *Days of Hope*, are melodramas of protest.

94 Quoted by Paget in '*Cathy Come Home* and "Accuracy" in British Television Drama', p. 76.

95 Sandford, DVD commentary.

96 Sandford, *Cathy Come Home*, p. 24.

97 Ibid., p. 17.

98 Ibid., p. 18.

99 Sandford, 'Edna and Cathy'.

100 Jeremy Sandford, 'Warp-aftermath of Cathy 2', <www.JeremySandford.org.uk> (last accessed 24 March 2009).

101 Loach, DVD commentary.

102 Sandford, Cathy Come Home (screenplay), p. 48.

103 Ibid., p. 49.

104 Sandford, DVD commentary.

105 Caughie, *Television Drama*, pp. 119–20.

106 Jacob Leigh, *The Cinema of Ken Loach: Art in the Service of the People* (London: Wallflower Press, 2002), p. 23.

107 Quoted in Lacey, *Tony Garnett*, p. 43 (emphasis in original).

108 Caughie, *Television Drama*, p. 123.

109 The letter comes from 1999, is titled <jeremycf-madeleine.html> and can be accessed via <www.JeremySandford. org.uk> (last accessed 6 March 2010).

110 BBC WAC T5/695/2, Memo from John Henderson.

111 For further discussion of this see Lacey, *British Realist Theatre*, especially chapter 6; Andrew Higson, 'Space, Place and Spectacle', *Screen* no. 4/5, 1984, pp. 2–21; and John Hill, *Sex, Class and Realism: British Cinema 1956–63* (London: BFI, 1986).

112 Quoted in Higson, 'Space, Place and Spectacle', p. 2.

113 These are transcribed from the DVD and do not appear in the published script.

114 Sandford, 'Warp-aftermath of Cathy 2'.

115 Loach, on DVD commentary.

116 See Leigh, *The Cinema of Ken Loach*, and Corner *The Art of Record*.

117 Wilson, *I Know it was the Place's Fault*, p. 18.

118 Transcribed from the DVD. All subsequent quotations are from the DVD rather than the published script to minimise discrepancies.

119 BBC WAC T5/695/1 VR/66/629, 'Audience Research Report: CATHY COME HOME', 6 December 1966.

120 See John Caughie, 'What do Actors do when they Act?', in Jonathan Bignell, Stephen Lacey and Madeleine MacMurraugh-Kavanagh (eds), *British Television Drama: Past, Present and Future* (Basingstoke: Palgrave/Macmillan, 2000); John Adams, 'Screen Play: Elements of a Performance Aesthetic in Television Drama', in J. Ridgman (ed.), *Boxed Sets* (Hadleigh: University of Luton Press/Arts Council of England, 1998); Kim Durham, 'Methodology and Praxis of the Actor within the Television Production Process: Facing the Camera in EastEnders and Inspector Morse', *Studies in Theatre and Performance* vol. 22 no. 22, 2002; Christine Cornea (ed.), *Genre and Performance: Film and Television* (Manchester: Manchester University Press, 2010).

121 For a succinct discussion of Kuleshov's arguments see Paul MacDonald, 'Why Study Film Acting? Some Opening Reflections', in Cynthai Baron, Diane Carson and Frank P. Tomasulo (eds), *More Than a Method* (Detroit: Wayne State University Press, 2004).

122 Ken Loach, interviewed by Jeremy Isaacs, *Face to Face*, BBC2 (19 September 1994).

123 Fuller and Loach, *Loach on Loach*, p. 6.
124 Loach, DVD commentary.
125 Ibid.
126 Ibid.
127 BBC WAC T5/695/2, Tony Garnett, Letter to Jean Diamond (London Management), 19 May 1966.
128 Jeremy Sandford, 'Warp-carol-first-meeting html' at <www.JeremySandford. org.uk> (accessed 5 August 2009).
129 Loach, DVD commentary.
130 Ken Loach, interviewed by Jeremy Isaacs, *Face to Face*.
131 Leigh, *The Cinema of Ken Loach*, p. 46.
132 Caughie, 'What do Actors do when they Act?', p. 166.
133 Maddison, 'What is a Television Film?', p. 75.
134 Don Taylor, 'The Gorboduc Stage', *Contrast* vol. 3 no. 3, Spring 1964, p. 207.
135 See Richard Dyer, *Stars* (London: BFI, 1992).
136 Ibid., p. 17.
137 Interview with the author, 7 March 2005. Garnett has made this comment, or variations on it, on several occasions.
138 John Roberts, 'Carol White', *Classic Image* no. 139, January 1987, p. 15.
139 Shubik, *Play for Today*, p. 113.
140 Paget, *True Stories*, p. 96.
141 Sandford, Cathy Come Home, p. 13.
142 Quoted in Paget, '*Cathy Come Home* and "Accuracy" in British Television Drama', p. 84.
143 Sandford, DVD commentary.
144 Usher, untitled, *Daily Sketch*.
145 Robert MacDonald, 'BBC Viewers to get "Agitational Drama"', *The Scotsman*, 17 August 1967.
146 Both articles published on 5 November 1965.
147 Ibid., p. 250.
148 Ibid., p. 254.

149 '*Cathy Come Home* press release', BBC WAC T5/695/1.
150 Ibid.
151 Gerard Fay, '*Cathy Come Home* on BBC1', *Guardian*, 17 November 1966.
152 Sylvia Clayton, 'Play's Plea for Homeless Families', *Daily Telegraph*, 17 November 1966.
153 Philip Purser, 'Black and White Play', *Sunday Telegraph*, 20 November 1966.
154 BBC WAC VR/66/629.
155 Peter Black, ibid.
156 John Gross, ibid.
157 Gerard Fay, ibid.
158 Peter Black, ibid.
159 Laurence Evans, 'What Cathy Did – and Did Not Do ...', *The Municipal and Public Services Journal*, 2 December 1966, p. 3972.
160 Ibid.
161 Brian Dean, 'Two Million Try to Trap "Cathy"', *Daily Mail*, 11 January 1967.
162 Celia Curtis, 'The Other Side of the Coin', interview with Alderman Frank Griffin, Leader of Birmingham City Council, *The Birmingham Post*, 17 November 1966.
163 Jeremy Sandford, 'What I Set Out to Do', and Linda Dyson, 'The Play as I Saw It', *The Birmingham Post*, 17 November 1966.
164 BBC WAC T5/695/1, Notes on Controller's Meeting, 29 November 1966.
165 BBC WAC T5/695/1, Garnett memo to HDG Television, 'Meeting at the Ministry of Housing: "Cathy Come Home"', 1 December 1966.
166 Ibid.
167 Ibid.
168 BBC WAC T5/695/2, 'CATHY COME HOME' memo from Gerald Savoury, Head of Plays, to Head of Overseas Sales, 16 December 1966.
169 Quoted in Alan Rosenthal, *The Documentary Conscience: A Casebook in*

127

Film Making (Berkeley: University of California Press, 1980), p. 161.

170 Robert Wright Cooper, ' "Cathy" Repeat Justifies its Dramatic Validity', *The Times*, 12 January 1967.

171 Paget, 'Cathy Come Home and "Accuracy" in British Television Drama'.

172 See Jeremy Sandford 'Cathy-trash 1' at <www.JeremySandford.org.uk> (accessed on 19 March 2009).

173 Shubik, *Play for Today*.

174 Both published on 11 January 1967.

175 *Daily Mirror*, 11 January 1967.

176 Madeleine MacMurraugh-Kavanagh, ' "Drama" into "News": Strategies of Intervention in "The Wednesday Play" ', *Screen* vol. 38 no. 3, Autumn 1997, pp. 367–81.

177 James Green, 'BBC Axe Potter's "Black" Cinderella', *Evening News*, 6 December 1966.

178 Philip Phillips, 'TV "Alice" Snubbed by Millions', *Sun*, 10 January 1967.

179 James Thomas, 'Loaded, But it Hurt Like Mad', *Daily Express*, 12 January 1967.

180 Unsigned, ' "Cathy" Repeat Justifies its Dramatic Validity', *The Times*, 12 January 1967.

181 Ibid.

182 Stanley Reynolds, 'Television', *Guardian*, 12 January 1967.

183 BBC WAC T5/695/1 VR/67/27, BBC Audience Research Report, CATHY COME HOME repeat screening, 1 February 1967.

184 Ibid.

185 All quotations from Wyndham Goldie are from this article.

186 Goodwin, A., P. Kerr and I. McDonald (eds), *BFI Dossier 19: Drama-Documentary* (London: BFI, 1983), p. 2.

187 'Full page advertisement for Shelter', obtained from *Guardian*, 12 January 1967: BBC WAC T5/695/1 (emphasis in original).

188 Wilson, *I Know it was the Place's Fault*.

189 Ibid., p. 238.

190 <england.shelter.org.uk/about_us/who_ we_are/our_history> (accessed 12 January 2010).

191 Bruce Kenrick, 'Cathy Can Come Home', *Evening News*, 16 January 1967.

192 Quoted in Wilson, *I Know it was the Place's Fault*, p. 19.

193 Ibid., p. 20 (emphasis in original).

194 Jeremy Sandford, letter to Gerald Savoury, 26 October 1968, BBC WAC T5/695/1.

195 There are several accounts of this period of post-war history, especially intellectual history: see Seed's 'Hegemony Postponed'. For an account of the effect of British Trotskyism on Loach and Garnett, see Lacey, *Tony Garnett*.

196 G. Roy Levin 'Tony Garnett and Kenneth Loach', *Documentary Explorations: 15 Interviews with Film-makers* (New York: Doubleday, 1971), p. 101.

197 Ibid.

198 Loach and Fuller, *Loach on Loach*, p. 24.

199 Ibid., pp. 101–2.

200 Interview with the author, 7 March 2005.

Bibliography

Adams, John, 'Screen Play: Elements of a Performance Aesthetic in Television Drama', in J. Ridgman (ed.), *Boxed Sets* (Hadleigh: University of Luton Press/Arts Council of England, 1998).

BBC WAC T5/695/1, *Cathy Come Home*; introduction to the storyline for *The Abyss*, 28 January 1965.

— T5/695/2, Memo from John Henderson (Assistant Head of Copyright) to Ken Loach's agent, Jean Diamond (London Management), 19 April 1966.

— T5/695/1 VR/66/629, 'Audience Research Report: CATHY COME HOME', 6 December 1966.

— T5/695/2, 'CATHY COME HOME', memo from Gerald Savoury, Head of Plays, to Head of Overseas Sales, 16 December 1966.

— T5/695/1 VR/67/27, BBC 'Audience Research Report, CATHY COME HOME' repeat screening, 1 February 1967.

— T5/695/1, Notes on Controller's Meeting, 29 November 1966.

— T5/695/1, Tony Garnett memo to HDG Television, 'Meeting at the Ministry of Housing: "Cathy Come Home"', 1 December 1966.

— T5/695/2, Tony Garnett, Letter to Jean Diamond (London Management), 19 May 1966.

— T5/695/1: Shelter advert, *Guardian*, 12 January 1967.

Black, Peter, 'If Cathy Made You Think Last Night', *Daily Mail*, Thursday, 12 January 1967.

Bogdanor, Vernon, and Robert Skidelsky (eds), *The Age of Affluence: 1951–64* (Basingstoke: Macmillan, 1970).

Bryant, Steve, *The Television Heritage* (London: BFI, 1989).

Caughie, John, *Television Drama: Realism, Modernism and British Culture* (Oxford: Oxford University Press, 2000).

—, 'What do Actors do when they Act?', in Jonathan Bignell, Stephen Lacey and Madeleine MacMurraugh-Kavanagh (eds), *British Television Drama: Past, Present and Future* (Basingstoke: Palgrave/Macmillan, 2000), pp. 162–74.

—, Edge of Darkness (London: BFI, 2007).

Clayton, Sylvia, 'Play's Plea for Homeless Families', *Daily Telegraph*, 17 November 1966.

Cook, John, 'Between Grierson and Barnum: Sydney Newman and The Development of the Single Television Play at the BBC 1963–7', *Journal of British Cinema and Television* no. 2, Spring 2005, pp. 211–25.

Cooke, Lez, *British Television Drama: A History* (London: BFI, 2003).

—, 'Style, Technology and Innovation in British Television Drama', *Journal of British Cinema and Television* vol. 2 no. 1, July 2005, pp. 82–99.

Cornea, Christine, *Genre and Performance: Film and Television* (Manchester: Manchester University Press, 2010).

Corner, John, *The Art of Record: A Critical Introduction to Documentary* (Manchester University Press, 1996).

Curtis, Celia, 'The Other Side of the Coin', interview with Alderman Frank Griffin, Leader of Birmingham City Council, *The Birmingham Post*, 17 November 1966.

Dean, Brian, 'Two Million Try to Trap "Cathy"', *Daily Mail*, 11 January 1967.

Durham, Kim, 'Methodology and Praxis of the Actor within the Television Production Process: Facing the Camera in EastEnders and Inspector Morse', *Studies in Theatre and Performance* vol. 22 no. 22, 2002.

Dyer, Richard, *Stars* (London: BFI, 1992).

Dyson, Linda, 'The Play as I Saw It', *The Birmingham Post*, 17 November 1966.

Evans, Laurence, 'What Cathy Did – and Did Not Do ...', *The Municipal and Public Services Journal*, 2 December 1966, p. 3972.

Fay, Gerald, 'Cathy Come Home on BBC1', *Guardian*, 17 November 1966.

Fiske, John and John Hartley, *Reading Television* (London: Routledge, 2003).

Fuller, Graham and Ken Loach, *Loach on Loach* (London: Faber and Faber, 1998).

Garnett, Tony, 'Contexts', in Jonathan Bignell, Stephen Lacey and Madeleine MacMurraugh-Kavanagh (eds), *British Television Drama: Past, Present and Future* (Basingstoke: Palgrave/ Macmillan, 2000).

—, Letter, *Encore* no. 49, May–June 1964, p. 45.

Geraghty, Christine 'Classic Television: A Matter of Time', *Critical Studies in Television* vol. 4 no. 2, Autumn 2009, pp. 108–9.

Goodwin, A., P. Kerr and I. McDonald (eds), *BFI Dossier 19: Drama-Documentary* (London: BFI, 1983).

Green, James, 'BBC Axe Potter's "Black" Cinderella', *Evening News*, 6 December 1966.

Hare, David 'How the BBC Killed the TV Play', *The Times*, 25 August 2008.

Higson, Andrew, 'Space, Place and Spectacle', *Screen* no. 4/5, 1984, pp. 2–21.

Hill, John, *Sex, Class and Realism: British Cinema 1956–63* (London: BFI, 1986).

Kennedy Martin, Troy, 'Nats Go Home: First Statement of a New Drama for Television', *Encore* no. 48, March–April 1964, pp. 21–33.

Kenrick, Bruce, 'Cathy Can Come Home', *Evening News*, 16 January 1967.

Knight, Deborah, 'Naturalism, Narration and Critical Perspective: Ken Loach and the Experimental Method', in George McKnight (ed.), *Agent of Challenge and Defiance: The Films of Ken Loach* (Trowbridge: Flick, 1997), pp. 60–81.

Lacey, Stephen, *British Realist Theatre: The New Wave in its Context 1956–65* (London: Routledge, 1995).

—, 'Becoming Popular: Some Reflections on the Relationship Between Television and Theatre', in Jonathan Bignell and Stephen Lacey (eds), *Popular Television Drama: Critical Perspectives* (Manchester: Manchester University Press, 2005).

—, *Tony Garnett* (Manchester: Manchester University Press, 2007).

Laing, Stuart, *Representations of Working-Class Life 1957–1964* (Basingstoke: Macmillan, 1986).

Leigh, Jacob, *The Cinema of Ken Loach: Art in the Service of the People* (London: Wallflower Press, 2002).

Levin, G. Roy, 'Tony Garnett and Kenneth Loach', *Documentary Explorations: 15 Interviews with Film-makers* (New York: Doubleday, 1971), pp. 98–110.

Loach, Ken, commentary on DVD, *Cathy Come Home* (BBC Worldwide, 2003).

MacDonald, Paul, 'Why Study Film Acting? Some Opening Reflections', in Cynthai Baron, Diane Carson and Frank P. Tomasulo (eds), *More Than a Method* (Detroit: Wayne State University Press, 2004), pp. 23–41.

MacDonald, Robert, 'BBC Viewers to get "Agitational Drama"', *The Scotsman*, 17 August 1967.

Mackenzie, John, 'When Cathy Comes to Town', Project No. 2116/4369, BBC WAC T5/695/2.

MacMurraugh-Kavanagh, Madeleine, 'The BBC and the Birth of "The Wednesday Play", 1962–66: Institutional Containment Versus "Agitational Contemporaneity"', *Historical Journal of Film, Radio and Television* vol. 17 no. 3, 1997, pp. 367–81.

—, '"Drama" into "News": Strategies of Intervention in "The Wednesday Play"', *Screen* vol. 38 no. 3, Autumn 1997, pp. 247–59.

—, 'Kicking Over the Traces: An Interview with Tony Garnett', *Media Education Journal* vol. 24, Summer, 1998, pp. 23–30.

—, and Stephen Lacey, 'Who Framed Theatre?: The "Moment of Change" in Television Drama', *New Theatre Quarterly* no. 57, February 1999, pp. 58–74.

Maddison, John, 'What is a Television Film?', *Contrast* vol. 13 no. 1, Autumn 1963, pp. 7–9, 71–5.

McGrath, J. (1977) 'Television Drama: The Case against Naturalism', *Sight & Sound* vol. 46 no. 2, pp. 100–5.

Moore-Gilbert, Bart, and John Seed (eds), *Cultural Revolution? The Challenge of the Arts in the 1960s* (London: Routledge, 1992).

Newman, Sydney, 'The Wednesday Play', Memo to Kenneth Adam, 15 June 1966, BBC WAC T5/695/2, 3798/9.

Paget, Derek, *True Stories?: Documentary Drama on Radio, Screen and Stage* (Manchester: Manchester University Press, 1990).

—, '*Cathy Come Home* and "Accuracy" in British Television Drama', *New Theatre Quarterly* no. 57, February 1999, pp. 58–74.

—, 'Preface' to Jeremy Sandford, Cathy Come Home (London: Marion Boyars, 2003).

Phillips, Philip, 'TV Alice Sunbbed by Millions', *Sun*, 10 January 1967.

Pinto-Duschinsky, Michael, 'Bread and Circuses? The Conservatives in Office, 1951–64', in Vernon Bogdanor and Robert Skidelsky (eds), *The Age of Affluence: 1951–64* (Basingstoke: Macmillan, 1970), pp. 55–77.

Purser, Philip, 'Black and White Play', *Sunday Telegraph*, 20 November 1966.

Quart, Leonard, 'A Fidelity to the Real: An Interview with Ken Loach and Tony Garnett', *Cineaste* no. 4, Autumn, pp. 26–9.

Reynolds, Stanley, 'Television', *Guardian*, 12 January 1967.

Roberts, John, 'Carol White', *Classic Image* no. 139, January 1987, pp. 15–16.

Rolinson, Dave 'Play for Today' <www.britishtelevisiondrama.org.uk/playfortoday/> (accessed 12 March 2010).

Rosenthal, Alan, *The Documentary Conscience: A Casebook in Film Making* (Berkeley: University of California Press, 1980).

Sandford, Jeremy, 'What I Set Out to Do', *The Birmingham Post*, 17 November 1966.

—, *Cathy Come Home: The Novel* (London: Pan, 1967).

—, letter to Gerald Savoury, 26 October 1968, BBC WAC T5/695/1.

—, 'Edna and Cathy: Just Huge Commercials', *Theatre Quarterly* vol. 3 no. 10, 1973, pp. 79–85.

—, Cathy Come Home (London: Marion Boyars, 1976, reprinted 2003).

131

—, commentary on the DVD extras, *Cathy Come Home* (BBC Worldwide, 2003).

—, 'Cathy-trash 1' at <www.JeremySandford.org.uk> (accessed 19 March 2009).

—, 'The Trashing of Cathy', <www.JeremySandford.org.uk> (accessed 24 March 2009).

—, 'Warp-Aftermath of Cathy', at <www.JeremySandford.org.uk> (accessed 24 March 2009).

—, 'Warp-aftermath of Cathy 2', <www.JeremySandford.org.uk> (accessed 24 March 2009).

—, 'Warp-carol-first-meeting html' at <www.JeremySandford.org.uk> (accessed 5 August 2009).

—, <jeremycf-madeleine.html> at <www.JeremySandford.org.uk> (accessed 6 March 2010).

Scannell, Paddy, 'The Social Eye of Television, 1946–1955', *Media, Culture and Society* vol. 1 no. 1. 1979, pp. 97–106.

Seed, John, 'Hegemony Postponed: The Unravelling of Consensus in Britain in the 1960s', in Bart Moore-Gilbert and John Seed (eds), *Cultural Revolution? The Challenge of the Arts in the 1960s* (London: Routledge, 1992), pp. 15–44.

Sexton, Jamie, ' "Televerite" hits Britain: Documentary, Drama and the Growth of 16mm Filmmaking in British Television', *Screen* vol. 44 no. 4, Winter 2003, pp. 429–44.

Shapiro, Sally, 'Town Hall Check on Play That Shocked', *Daily Sketch*, 11 January 1967.

Shelter, <england.shelter.org.uk/about_us/ who_we_are/our_history> (accessed 12 January 2010).

Shubik, Irene, *Play for Today: The Evolution of Television Drama*, 2nd edn (Manchester: Manchester University Press, 2000).

Taylor, Don, 'The Gorboduc Stage', *Contrast* vol. 3 no. 3, Spring 1964, pp. 151–3, 204–8.

Thomas, James, 'Loaded, But it Hurt Like Mad', *Daily Express*, 12 January 1967.

Unsigned, ' "Cathy" Repeat Justifies its Dramatic Validity', *The Times*, 12 January 1967.

Usher, Shaun, untitled, *Daily Sketch*, 17 August 1966.

Walker, Michael, 'Melodrama and the American Cinema', *Movie* no. 29/30, Summer 1982, pp. 2–38.

Williams, Raymond, 'Recent English Drama', in B. Ford (ed.), *The Pelican Guide to English Literature No. 7: The Modern Age* (London: Pelican, 1978).

—, *Politics and Letters* (London: New Left, 1979).

—, 'A Defence of Realism', in Williams, *What I Came to Say* (London: Hutchinson Radius, 1990), pp. 226–39.

Wilson, Des, *I Know it was the Place's Fault* (London: Oliphant, 1970).

Wright Cooper, Robert, ' "Cathy" Repeat Justifies its Dramatic Validity', *The Times*, 12 January 1967.

Wyndham Goldie, Grace, 'Stop Mixing TV Fact and Fiction', *Sunday Telegraph*, 8 January 1967.

Credits

Cathy Come Home

Great Britain/1966

directed by
Kenneth Loach
producer
Tony Garnett
a story by
Jeremy Sandford
camera
Tony Imi
editor
Roy Watts
designer
Sally Hulke
sound
Malcolm Campbell

Production Company
BBC TV

uncredited
writer
Kenneth Loach
costumes
Valerie Spooner
music
Paul Jones

cast
Carol White
Cathy Ward
Ray Brooks
Reg Ward
Winifred Dennis
Mrs Ward
Wally Patch
Grandad
Adrienne Frame
Eileen
Emmett Hennessy
Johnny
Alec Coleman
wedding guest
Geoffrey Palmer
property agent
Gabrielle Hamilton
welfare office

Phyllis Hickson
Mrs Alley
Frank Veasey
Mr Hodge
Barry Jackson
rent collector
James Benton
man at eviction
Ruth Kettlewell
judge
John Baddeley
housing officer
Kathleen Broadhurst
landlady
Ralph Lawton
health inspector

in the caravans
Gladys Dawson
Mrs Penfold
Ronald Pember
Mr Jones
Paddy Joyce
Mr Abercander
Liz McKenzie
Mrs Jones
Maureen Ampleford
Pauline Jones
Anne Ayres
Anne Jones

the ratepayers
Lennard Pearce
David Crane
Alan Selwyn

sleeping rough
Will Stampe
boat proprietor
Geraldine Moon
girl in derelict house
Bernard Price
man in street

at the Cumbermere Lodge
Charles Leno
warden
John Lawrence
welfare committee member
Joan Harsant
nurse
Faith Kent
welfare committee member

inmates at Cumbermere Lodge
Julie May
Myrtle McKenzie
Patti Dalton
Rose Hiller
Paddy Kent

at Holm Lea
Cleo Sylvestre
Terri Ansell
Andrea Lawrence
Doreen Herrington
Muriel Hunte
inmates
Edwin Brown
warden
Helen Booth
landlady
Lila Kaye
staff
Anne Hardcastle
welfare woman

production
Filmed on location in
Hammersmith (London, GB).
16mm; black and white.

First shown on BBC1 on 16
November 1966 as part of
series The Wednesday Play.
Running time: 76 minutes 50
seconds.

133

Index

Page numbers in **bold** indicate detailed analysis; those in *italic* denote illustrations.
n = endnote.

137

Also Published:

Buffy the Vampire Slayer	**The Office**
Anne Billson	Ben Walters
Civilisation	**Our Friends in the North**
Jonathan Conlin	Michael Eaton
Cracker	**Prime Suspect**
Mark Duguid	Deborah Jermyn
CSI: Crime Scene Investigation	**Queer as Folk**
Steven Cohan	Glyn Davis
Doctor Who	**Seinfeld**
Kim Newman	Nicholas Mirzoeff
Edge of Darkness	**Seven Up**
John Caughie	Stella Bruzzi
Law and Order	**The Singing Detective**
Charlotte Brunsdon	Glen Creeber
The League of Gentlemen	**Star Trek**
Leon Hunt	Ina Rae Hark
The Likely Lads	
Phil Wickham	